HELP ME

By

MEL BOWERS

ISBN NUMBER - 0692045902

Table of Contents

INTRODUCTION

A s I took my morning walk doing my daily exercise I talked with God as I do every day. I had gotten into this routine while pregnant that only allowed alone time with God. I'd text the daily devotion to my friends, shoot a text that I'm headed for my walk for safety reasons and start my day. For myself I'm always glued to my phone, but during this time no phone was allowed. One day as I walked I saw a mirror on a front porch inscribed with what looked like blood that read: 'Help me' I was immediately startled by what I saw for many reasons. My mind went all over the place. This wasn't normal. Why was it there? Was someone in a Discovery ID Channel situation? Or was I over reacting. Honestly this could be a real cry for help with someone being in danger. Hear me when I say this wasn't your normal porch greeting and I had to decide what to do. Do I call for help just to be sure everyone was safe, or do I just mind my own business and lift the home owners in prayer? It would bother me later to my core had I witnessed something was wrong at this home on the five o'clock news and I didn't call for help. I saw a man coming my way, he would help I'm sure. As I explained the situation he said, "Oh its fine" and kept walking. Nevertheless, I decided to keep walking as well and I'd re-check the situation the next day. The next day brought no change. Maybe this was a Halloween prank gone wrong. Seemed to me everything was fine, and at this moment it was clear the Holy Spirit was speaking to me letting me see everything is fine in the home. But, is everything well with you? Is there anything you know you need to be helped with?

I was deeply moved by this mirror and its inscription, it seemed the Holy Spirit was screaming this message was just for you. You need to get on the ball, write the book, you're an author and here is the title. I'm the child who must be burned on the hot stove to know it's hot. Meaning God has to show me clearly to really get it. That very second it hit me I wasn't only birthing a new baby, but it was time to be obedient and birth other things as well. This was no surprise to me, I knew it was way overdue. I had so much on my heart, so much to say and most of all I knew the inscription wasn't only for me but so many in need of Help. Others were seeing the mirror on the porch in my mind and needed a help guide to be set free. I couldn't abort this opportunity. I had a visual and I knew that it was just for me. Now, it was my time to not only cry out for me but for those who are suffering silently every day. The ones who may never walk past this house and see the porch greeting. For those who I needed to become their voice of reason to help themselves be better. I was here for it and was ready. Thus, that inscription became the title of my book. Here we Grow!

Chapter 1

A s I reviewed my thoughts about what I had seen on the porch, went over my life, and all that had been spoken over my life in the past I had a clear revelation of the Holy Spirit. I knew it was my time to walk in my destiny and my anointing with my book. Not only had I gone through a ton secretly in my life, but publicly. The fact that I could be transparent and help others discover where they sought help in their lives gave me a new song to sing. Well not literally but it gave me hope that I was going to help someone heal. If I could help one person admit their pain, issues or hurt I was on the ball. And boy was I ready to sing. I know that people act as if they want help, but at times get it from those who won't tell them the truth. For me to write this book it would allow others to read my testimony and see for themselves where their issues lie.

Now, I knew I had to get to work. But, before I began God sent a confirmation through a stranger who told me that it was time for my book to come forth, it was not a time to be disobedient and it would help people all over the nation. See, you must know yourself and boy do I know me. I knew a few things for sure about myself, one being that I am a procrastinator on things that I'm unsure of or afraid of. I'm a risk taker and I don't mind trying and failing. One other thing I'm aware of is that I quit when I become bored or uninterested and honestly that was often with my life. Some may say I have ADD when it comes to business, ideas and getting to the money. Myself like so many others completing task due to busy life, laziness and being afraid. But it hit me

"Girl your thoughts will never manifest to the nations if you don't get started".

Were often so afraid of commitment and failure that it causes us to play hide and seek with our dreams. We want it but we won't just go for it. We do things for a few days, weeks, months and we quit if we don't see the reward quick. We could know its purposed just for us. We can feel it's our destiny and we will still stop short of the finish line. But, this wasn't the answer for the book. This book would explain so much about me, it would help others to overcome and most of all show how I left the devils army and joined the fight for Christ. Let's be clear this book isn't to try and prove perfection but to exhibit my true walk with Jesus flaws and all.

People feel they must be perfect and walk a straight line never messing up to be a Christian. But, this is far from true. I am who I am and best of all Jesus knows it and me. He knows I'm far from perfect and I will still cut the buck here and there. I love to have fun and will fall and seek His help in getting back up. But, I also know that in the walk I've grown, matured and I seek to be more like Christ daily. I really put in an effort and I've seen what He's done for me for myself. And, most of all nobody can change how I feel because of my own firsthand experiences.

Recently with my life's experiences I've been forced to realize that life doesn't always go as planned, it's not always easy, Gods plans aren't always ours and most of all we must deal with it. I know for a fact that the world will continue spinning no matter how hard it gets. No matter how many times we desire to quit or give up. Or the struggles we face. So, it's clear we must continue pressing or give up and giving up isn't an option for me. I feel that its best that we don't know Gods every move or plan for our lives. The reason being is because some of us would revamp Gods plan with ours and never see His manifest. The more profound thing these days is there's so much going on that it's a constant influence on how we do things. How we dress, the cars we drive, how we do our hair, how we wear beards and so on. The hatred, dysfunction, murders, abuse daily and negative is also an influence on our feelings and emotions. To top it all off we see so many people dying daily, and it seems its younger and younger and in harsh manners. Talk about a reality check. Death seems to consume us daily. I have some close friends who have lost children and suffered, this shows that God is not a respecter of person. He giveth and he can take away. I just don't know if I could bare that. Often, we forget it all belongs to Him and he has free will with our lives. His word and works apply to us all and none of us are exempt from life's trials and tribulations.

Before I began writing this book I was confused about which part of my life to start writing about, so I asked myself: "How do I start?" "Where do I begin?" Is it the hurt experienced, the abandonment, the great entrepreneur in me, the depression, the confusion, being a mom, not having a relationship with my biological mom, the bad relationships, the marriage, the divorce, losing so much, the federal case, my undisclosed hurt, the gains, the friendships, the friends who became enemies, never wanting to be alone? Sheesh! This list was getting too long. So, I stopped and asked God what He wanted his people to hear. His instant response was, "Your heart". Instantly I said that's it my heart. But, what did that mean exactly? If I spoke from my heart you'd get all sides of my life, the good, the bad and the ugly. One thing for sure is that my readers would get the transparent me. Something that would heal and set free. That's what God wanted. This couldn't just be another book on a shelf, but a testimony to how far God had brought me.

I've done some wonderful things in life and some not so wonderful things. I've suffered losses, I've gained, mistreated, lied, cheated, gotten over, been a lossy friend, bad lover, a hater and so on and so forth. I've done a lot and learned enough to want to share the real to help someone see they can make it. The wonderful thing about this is I've been delivered somewhat from "Peopleism", which means from peoples chatter about me. I could write this book and be honest and worry about those it helped verses those who would talk and never buy it and read it.

This was clear that we miss a lot of opportunities because of what people have to say. But, they could talk but this book was coming.

I realize that as we go through life we experience so much that has an impact on how we grow, some of these experiences grow us and some stunt our growth. Though a lot of our experiences can be a major part of why as humans we become walking disasters and shipwrecks. The hurt, pain, break ups, lies, parents, divorces, people, lust and so and much more. But, the horrible part is that we begin to learn early how to cover it up within our usual roles. It becomes our normal flow. We teach our boys that crying is weak, men can't be emotional. We allow music, sports, video games, television, social media, electronic devices and tennis shoes to become major influencers. We advise our males not to show a weak side it's not right or cool to do so. We often teach them how to mask how they really feel or desire to be. Our daughters develop 'an attitude' to hide their feelings, play the role of the man, and even use their bodies to get what they want. This starts early and it's sad because whatever we start during childhood typically continues or resurfaces when we become adults. The patterns of dysfunction start so early it becomes our normal walk in life.

Stop... Let's go back. Let's consider our childhoods. Look at the way you behave now, and how you handle issues and situations. How do you respond, communicate and correspond? After evaluating your habits most likely you'll see some familiarities that may indicate you've been a jacked-up mess for a long time. It's nothing to be ashamed of because many of us are a mess. What many of us need to do is a Metox, and that's the purpose of this book. You may ask what a Metox is? It's a self-detox, a detox for the inner of you. This process is to help us self-discover our issues and get through them with some self-help.

The start of our issues often come from us not being honest with who we are, our deeply rooted issues, and what has us suffering. We tend to lie to the very person we should be honest with and that's ourselves. It's easy to lie to others but when it comes to evaluating your life and not wanting to be honest with self this is an issue. Some steps to be a better you are evicting some of the old you, old ways, old issues and starting over with the new you. To be a better you we must stop and drop some things, some people, some habits, some hurt and some us. Some of our ways don't fit us any longer. Some of the people you hang with can't go where you're going. Somethings we haven't evicted are holding us at an address we no longer reside or don't want to any longer. Maybe it's the fact that we haven't sat to evaluate where we are now verse where we were. Self-evaluations of your life are necessary and more often than we think. It's like a life physical but you're the doctor you're checking to see what needs help, some and you write the prescription for your healing and recovery. The Important thing about this is you don't have to tell or share your illness with anyone but you. Unless you see fit that what you have going on needs a deeper look. This allows you to heal without a lot of clutter or chatter. Your issues can't always be helped by your friends or family. Some stuff you must do for you.

Help Me Some Stuff must GO…

Chapter 2

I was born on Dec 8th, 1982 and my story till date will make you believe in God. I can take you on a roller coaster ride, through a hurricane, show you a few rainbows, and then bring you to a happy place. I'll never complain or even try to change my story because it's perfect for me. Honestly in my weakness I've witnessed God as my strength on so many parts of my life. My roadblocks have only been a re-route for my growth and the tears have allowed my release in so many tough situations. I know for a fact that I feel I'm being groomed for a greater stage, a stage where my testimony will bless lives to see they can make it through their storms. I believe God needs some notable examples to his work so others can see a visual of how grand He is. I'm also a visual person so often I need to see a sample. So many of us doubt what we can't see. So, I feel he uses me often so people can see an example of his power and what he's capable of doing for those who don't believe.

I realize that everything that damaged me and tried to break me was for this moment. It was so I could be a true witness to why we all can ask for help. This was for me to not just speak on it from what I heard, but to speak from real life experiences. So, often I wanted to give up, many times I felt like I couldn't take life. Now, I know I'm a true example of why you can and will make it. Really the decision is yours, it's up to us to get up and make the changes in ourselves that will only help us to be better. It can't be don't by force but by choice.

Being born into this world is supposed to be a blessing, and it will forever be that for me. But, from the beginning I had reasons to look back at what made me cry out for "Help." Let's look at my childhood. In our society, being raised by a mother is prevalent to being raised by a father. But, in my case my dad and step mom raised me, let me be clear they were great parents. Providers, teachers, they loved and disciplined me. I am who I am because of them. Nevertheless, it was a personal issue from an early age that caused issues. I feel I masked it or tried to pretend it was never a bother because of how amazing my dad was to me. Never would I want to hurt him or play down his sacrifice of being an amazing dad. Everyone who knows me can verify the love I have for my father, I eat, sleep and breathe love for my him. And, I'll always be thankful and forever grateful to them. I'm not saying they were perfect, but I realize they gave us what they had when raising us. Nevertheless, my cry for Help was always due to carrying a deep pain created because my biological mom wasn't there to raise me. As a young girl you just desire certain things, and being honest my stepmom wanted to do those things, but my wall was built to create a block, so I couldn't replace what I wanted from my mother. There were just things I felt I deserved growing up. To have intimate conversations with my mother was to me not too much to ask. My milestones she missed were tough for me. You know the "Hey mom "I'm on my cycle", "I fell off my bike", "I have a boothang" those type conversations. I know many may say you had a great step mom, get over it. My dad did remarry early on, but I didn't allow the relationship to evolve as I could have because I had personal issues. We often act out and do things that we really don't understand when were hurt. I know when I was younger I didn't know how to explain how I felt, but it was a feeling when that let me know something was wrong. I had a wall from the start to not allow a healthy relationship early because of who I was inside. I feel a mother is a major part of a child's life, the bond that's created in the womb is unexplainable. So, I had to wonder where did our bond go wrong, was there something I didn't know. Were there pieces of the puzzle that I just missed? Our Mothers are created to embed a huge imprint on our

13

lives. Nine whole months of bonding and growing together. If we look up what the number nine signifies is the perfect movement of God or to accomplish divine will. God could have said five months or seven months he gives us nine months to complete a perfect move of God. This is the time we get to know our children, begin to protect and care for them. I won't ever down play a father I just don't know what it's like to be one. I know many great fathers I had one. But, I must speak from experience. There are some amazing fathers in the world, big praise to you as well.

Many days I've wondered why God allowed women to carry children and not the father? This question has baffled me lately and has me pondering on the answer. Fathers roles are different than mothers in my opinion and this was with great intention from God. The miracle of parenthood is a blessing. To even look at how two people can conceive such a miracle is miraculous.

I now realize that this is where a lot of my pain lies. I feel it was the start of it anyway. This was also the start of many unhealthy habits. Seeking people and relationships from individuals who needed me more than I need them. Or being attracted to those who lack where I stand strong. In my mind my process of thinking was to attract people who wouldn't leave me. This is where the thought of leaving people before they left me was planted in my mind. This is where the phase of doubting and questioning myself at an early slid through the cracks. Note that when we leave a crack the enemy will slither in and will bite if were not careful. We must be conscious of allowing garbage to fill our space and poison to attack our system. Remember we are doing a Metox meaning we are dissecting our personal life and discovering how to take bandages off our scars and let them heal.

Currently our society doesn't know the importance of a healthy family structure or even a healthy co-parent relationship. We're adding new babies to the world like ticks on a board. Most often now days we jump into bed without stable intention. We don't even get to know our sex partners. See, some may say what does she mean don't know our sex partners? Well, knowing a person is more than a name, more than where you met them it, but who are we producing deeper than that. And if we look at statistics were doing an excellent job at reproducing, but what are we producing. We often do this without protection and no desire to be with the person were sleeping. Many are just seeking an enjoyable time. So where does this leave children that are conceived during sexcapades? The answer is in single parent homes. It's the start of the broken cycle. Let me be clear and say sometimes being a single parent is inevitable and can't be avoided. I'm not saying being a single parent is a terrible thing or can't produce great children. What I am saying is it can create a void and abandonment issues that children may not realize. But, this can cause hurt to form at an early age. This same hurt can be there with both parents in the home. Just because two parents are in a home doesn't mean this is a healthy situation. Some families are only together because of children. There is nothing left period but a stable environment for the children. Just a situationship for the world and the child or children to see. One thing about children they are a lot smarter and observant than we realize, we must be careful of what we subject them to. The effects and hurt that adults can cause them. We can be a major growth and development issue. We also have to be careful of the decision we make for them as well, some of our adult decisions are the very reason many children are damaged, and we don't recognize it because we often do what's best for us verses the child.

No matter the reason children are left in a single parent home its can have an effect. Whether the parent left because of imprisonment, death, or just by choice, many children are left trying to figure their deep issues early. Children have needs they need love, to be taught, groomed, and disciplined. Their development stems from the things we give them daily. Imagine every holiday, birthday and milestone that my mom missed. Now take a healthy heart and chizzle out a piece every day and you realize that the days are no longer complete. You may begin to search for ways to fill in the broken pieces with other people and things, but it's not the same honestly. Some problems can only be managed but can't be solved – and that's our Help point. We become so accustomed to acting like it's not okay to feel hurt from life's issue's. When it is okay not to be okay sometimes and to even seek help. As a matter of fact, it's dire to a healthy life to go through some "stuff in life so it can build a stronger you after the storm.

I needed help and I didn't need to act like an issue didn't exist. Let's not play the blame game. I wouldn't dare blame my mother because I'm thankful for her decision to have me, and for my parents to come to a decision that he would raise men I appreciate her so much more today, because she had the option to get rid of me and she decided to allow me to live. The life that she allowed has me where I am now. I can see now what I couldn't see then. It's like it was working for my good after all. But, I must now ask some real questions that can never be answered now. My mom passed in 2008 rest her soul. I've particularly been left to wonder how she was raised? What was her knowledge of being a mother of two girls? Did she experience motherly love growing up? Did she feel a void in her youth? What was on her heart for me and my well-being? We often feel like because a person was physically there they exhibit all the excellent traits of a parent. Just because you provide all that's needed and buy the latest name brands and now days post pictures on social media doesn't make you a stellar parent. Some parents relate money to being a great parent. Most often kids would take time and love over material things.

We jump to conclusions when we can't figure out the reasons behind someone's actions. Through the years, I've tried to understand it and I've also come to realize that God gave my dad a wife to fill some of the voids in my life. He knew way back id need an example of what a mother was even if I was unaccepting. He knew I wouldn't be open to have a healthy relationship due to having so much resentment in my heart. I was so angry and filled with pain that my heart was never open to receive her love. Indeed, as a child, I never knew that I was crying out for help. It made me develop a hard shell over my hard feelings. It's caused me to hurt others because I was hurt. But, we often cry out by perpetrating actions to avoid how we feel.

From childhood, we should incorporate a stable platform of communication with our kids. We should practice having some open conversations to see how they really feel. This can help us resolve issues a lot faster and teach them how important communication is. This leaves an open window for real conversations to be discussed at any time. No matter how beautiful or stable we may seem, living a life of pretense can cause mental imbalances. Just like a car with mechanical issues that's never repaired, it eventually quits, breaks down and becomes a waste. We must understand that our pain and problems need some repairing to have a balanced life. We must be honest to repair, but most times. We don't like to speak on issues or uncomfortable topics no matter how much it's needed. We don't like to seek help. We are accustomed to certain patterns, and we don't like resolving issues and moving on. We love to hide and cover up, hold and cover up and we don't take care of problems as they arise. And we then wonder why so many people, relationships, children, and marriages are in shambles. It's because we don't deal with problems we neglect them. HELP US...

Chapter 3

I'd never felt so lost, exhausted, or burnt out mentally in my life. It seemed my GPS had stopped working I could hear it saying reroute. Everything around me seemed to be slowly headed down a path of devastation. I had been pretending that I had it all together. I had become a professional pretender. I needed people to see pictures on social media and say she is doing good. Remember I lived for what people thought for a long time. I couldn't let go of this facade would, because if so it would lead me some where I hadn't been before and that was towards the truth. The truth was I had no direction, and it seemed that my prayers weren't getting past the ceiling. I was reaching for people, relationships, and sought approval from everyone that couldn't provide it. I felt secluded, and I was trying to get ahead through a medium that proved abortive for years. I felt I was carrying a heavy weight I was burdened on angry at the world. Not to mention the many nights of tears from the pressure of life I had cried. The reality of my life was becoming unbearable. All my life I heard you're so strong and now I needed someone to be strong for me. I never knew or realized that I could imprison myself with my issues and my past. The movie "Get Out" became a reality to me, as if the tea cup of life was being tapped, and I was sinking into a sunken place. I felt as if I were in a battle for my life. I was on a collision course, especially since so many people felt I had it all together. So many thought my life was well put together, I had perfected the art of pretending for the world. The sheet that I was using to cover my flaws and issues was slowly pulling off me. I was spiraling out of control, and no man, sex, food or relationship could fix it. Only God could deliver me, and I knew this. The need to be approved by people and trying to satisfy the on lookers more than being real with myself was killing me.

I began to ask "Where is God and why isn't He helping me get out of this dark place. And one day I got my answer. He was right where I left him. I had all the answers, I had it all figured out, I was something like a user of God. The remarkable thing about God is he knows how we are and still loves us through our mess. But, I kept crashing and running back to be rescued. I was good at putting God on the backseat until I needed him, and right when I was about to crash I ask Him to take the wheel. I can't recall a time he didn't. He was always right there to save me. He was there in all the times I had gotten myself in serious trouble. He was there when I was having unprotected sex to protect me from aids. He was there when money got low and I was about to be evicted with my boys. He never left me. I needed some answers for this storm, I didn't have it together at all. I was insecure, had low self-esteem, I had major trust issues and I needed approval from folks who didn't matter. I needed confirmation anything would do. I needed to have a dream, hear a song or a prophecy. I was in desperate need of God's touch, and I couldn't pretend anymore. I needed to be rerouted and be on the path that was created for me. I needed to be honest with myself and suddenly I concluded that I couldn't do this on my own. I began to ask questions like: "What is my purpose?" "Why was I even born?" "Who am I?" "What was the plan for my life. I started asking God what love was, who I was to him and what He saw in me. I needed to see his view for a change. I was desperate for change. I was becoming hopeless that life would be better. When you become desperate something it's at a sever place. I was in a humbling place. I desired His presence. I needed to feel his power. Because the way I was headed felt good on the outside, but the inside wasn't so great. I was really turning for the worse and I needed an Allstate plan, I needed to be in good hands. No just any man's hands for a change but Gods. I was losing stuff, almost homeless, had gotten in trouble, had an abortion by someone who I shouldn't have even had a conversation with. Not because of anything bad, but because we were different in our lives, thinking and overall mindset. I started to change I feel due to being in a weak state of mind. I need to be around people that were in that same state. I was hanging places I hadn't been before or even desired to. Hanging with people I didn't need and seeking answers that would appease this life I was living. Help Me I Need to hear your voice.

Chapter 4

S ometimes we get so caught up with what we and it causes us to lose sight on what we really need. Many of us suffer from identity crisis. Meaning we don't know who we really are. We go out and buy clothes, houses, and cars that we don't need to keep up with other people. We are often never satisfied with what we have no matter how good it is. We acquire bills that we can't afford to look good for people who can't afford them either. We like speeding in other people's lanes, with no clue of what all they had to do to stay in it. This my friend is an issue. This means that you have some traits of jealousy. When you begin to envy another person's life without cause. Now I may be being a bit harsh, but I must be honest. We as people need to truly check ourselves when it comes to minding another person's business. Let me be clear what another person has, lost, owns, rents, buys are for them to worry about and not you. We can't continue to be consumed by what other people have going on because we often live in a glass house and can't throw stones. If I was perfect and didn't have some flaws and issues, then I could talk but this isn't the case. We often try and hide our flows by running other people in the mud. It helps us to feel better about how horrible things are for us. If you ever get a chance to really see people's transparent lives you'd see issues and struggles that have them in state to want others to feel like them. Therefore, you must be careful with who and what you indulge in. Some things don't even deserve your response or time.

We can become so progressive and successful that we forget how blessed we are. How thankful we should be for where we are. So many people have it worse than we do, struggling with significant issues. Health issues that they can't be prevented. We forget the love that He has for us and how he has kept us. I think some of us need to experience struggle to be in a humbling situation. We can forget the times we didn't have having. We lose site of where we've been often because we have. But, stop and look at this. We didn't have to work for air, or the heart that pumps daily to keep you alive, or even the eyes that allow you to see or the legs and arms that function freely for you. Imagine not having any of this. Imagine having to function once you lose one. Things often mean more when you lose it. We have so much pride we care so much about things with so little significance. If you're anything like me then you may often complain and forget how good you have it. But, humble yourself and think about the people who have suffered. The ones with no food, or the man with no legs, or the blind girl, or the lady with cancer or the baby born with no arms, this can make you humble yourself. And, become a bit more appreciative. This tends to happen when my pride is on high. At times when I'm in a silent space and humble this is when I hear the Holy spirit. It's like we can't talk at the same time and I hear clearly. He began to speak to me when I decided to shut up. He allowed me to talk and try and figure my way out. He didn't force Himself on me. He needed me to get into posture to accept what he wanted me to hear. I had to be silent, had to fall on my knees, I could no longer care about people or what they would say or what they were doing, as He wanted all of me. I began to see my faith flip flop. He reminded me of all those times He had brought me out, carried me and handled what I didn't even have the mind to conquer. He showed me the things I desired more than Him and, how I was trying to be my own God. How I had the answers. He wanted me to be obedient and seek His word more than my desires and dreams. He knows how to get me to where I wanted to go He reassured me. But, was I willing to take the backseat. I realized that I couldn't keep driving down the road of demise. Because, it was this familiar road that kept taking me down the street of past hurts, fornication, broken relationships, church hurt, manipulation, financial distress, and dead ends. It seemed like I was deaf spiritually, but I was also going blind, and it made me spiritually handicap. Sometimes, we become deaf when we only want to hear what we want to hear from God, and what makes us happy and feels good. Typically, God's words make us uncomfortable and this disrupts Gods desires.

One thing about God He will never force us to listen or do anything. He is a compassionate God that gives us choices. Free will is the choice to do or say whatever we want to knowing that in life and with God comes consequences and repercussions. If you have children, you know as much as I do that you aren't willing to say the same thing repeatedly. But this is what we desire of God. We want to repeat our mistakes and escape punishment. God had been listening and speaking to me, the reality was He wasn't saying what I desired. I wanted to do things my way. Well, history has shown me that wasn't a good decision, Help Me to Hear You, Lord, because You Always Hear me!

Chapter 5

I must confess that so much of our lives, our steps and paths have been downloaded into us in a not so perfect manner. We've taken on direction and paths that have been detrimental to our growth. I feel with both men and women of all ethnicities there are so many hidden issues that we try and hide. We have people who are prejudice, pedophiles, sex addicts, drug addicts, rapist and have tons of other issues that you'd never guess. People get so use to secret dysfunction that we begin to function in it daily with no one ever knowing. People work normal jobs, have families, go to church all while secretly suffering from toxic behavior. Just imagine how many secrets you yourself hold from the world. The things you desire to take to your grave. This is everyone around you daily. You'd never know every detail about a person, and may would even be surprised to see some of what people hold inside daily. We live in a world where people expose and extort for likes on social media. We must be guarded and protect our image to be respected in society. We have women with the I don't need a man mindset. The miss independent, never want to be submissive attitude. We have men seeking a woman or multiple women to provide for them. People on social media becoming famous all through a few strikes on a keyboard. So many are depressed, stressed and suicidal. People who are one check away from being homeless are struggling. Not to mention this new age parenting. What in the heck is going on now days. I've never seen so much "Stuff" be approved by society. How we were raised, what we saw, and what we experienced has molded and had influence on how we function today. Little did you know every action of your guardian growing up was molding you into the person you daily.

Now, there are many significant issues I want to touch on in this chapter; generational curses, attachment issues and relationship dysfunction. I want to enlighten you on issues you may suffer from and never were aware. We will start with Generational curses. Generational curses are persistent and continual negative patterns of an events or occurrences that is something being handed down from generation to generation says google. Meaning people are dealing with issues that have been handed down from mom, grand mom, great grand mom, to great grandma. It could be the fact that you always struggle with addictions and many generations of your family were alcoholics and now you're suffering from it. You don't even have to have had a relationship with the family member to carry on the curses they suffer from. Genes is the start of generational curses. It's in a person genetics to carry on certain curses. High blood pressures, diabetes these are examples of generational curses.

Most Often people who were adopted, end up with the same characteristics as their birth parents, not because they were around their birth parents to learn how they behaved, but because they inherited their spiritual bondage and genes. Some common symptoms of generational curses are family illnesses that seem to just walk from one person down to the next (cancer is a common physical manifestation of a spiritual bondage), continual financial difficulties (they continually hit roadblocks in their finances), mental problems, persistent irrational fears, and depression. Anything that seems to be a continuing struggle or problem that was handed down from one generation to another may very well be a generational curse. We often down play generational issues and it can be a very serious issue that an individual suffers from. We don't always seek to know more about our past because were too busy trying to discover our future. We need to know our history to have a healthy future.

Next, we want to look at attachment issues it refers to deep connections established between a child and a guardian that affects the child's development and ability to express emotions and developing relationships. A person with insecure attachment or an attachment disorder lacks the skills for building meaningful relationships. Individuals with attachment disorders have difficulty connecting to others and managing their own emotions. This results in a lack of trust and self-worth, the fear of getting close to anyone is an issue, as well as the need to be in control. So why do some develop attachment disorders while others don't? The answer has to do with the attachment process, which relies on the interaction between a parent and child.

Attachment disorders are the result of bad experiences in early relationships. If children feel abandoned, isolated, alone, or uncared for, for whatever reason, they will learn that they can't depend on others and have trust issues as adults. This issue will continue typically in how we interact with other later in life. As I stated above we all must be aware of where the root of our issue lies to properly recognize them and heal.

Relationship dysfunction is a common issue for many of us. We jump from one person to the next without any sign of healing. It's hard to resist the repetition of a behavior when you don't understand why you keep doing it in the first place. We tend to deal with the same type of people and deal with the same type pain with a different face attached. We don't always know why we're willing to deal with what we deal with other than the fact that we do. We all have the choice to stay or leave and often we opt to stay no matter how terrible things get. This goes for friendships as well as dating.

All relationships are dysfunctional in diverse ways. No perfect relationships exist and if you know of one let me know. To stay in a committed relationship, most couples adapt to many disappointments and disillusionments during the dating phase. Depending on how the good outweighs the bad determines if one or both are willing to continue to fight for the relationship. But, if over time, you realize the bad days outweighed the good most likely after a while the strain of the drama can become a deal breaker. Significantly painful events that occur during that time can be deal breakers. Even initially 90% positive relationships can fail after too many broken promises or repeatedly unresolved conflicts or boundary issues. If cumulatively dysfunctional interactions occur, the relationship will not likely survive a major unpleasant situation. The more we act as if issues don't bother us and continue to have sex to fix issues the more likely it will end. Relationships can cause us issues in that we may never could have imagined even after the break up.

So many suffer from the issues above and have no clue. The funny aspect is we at times go to people who have no clue what we are suffering from and how bad. This book is not only for me, it's meant to help many discover the causes and effects of their problems. We are unaware of some of the deeply rooted issues that we suffer from, and what harm they are causing We tend to repeat unhealthy cycles. We continue walking down unhealthy paths because no one taught us different. Most often, we are also unware that we have been suffering as bad as many are. We've normalized and suffered for so long. And most times, we reach out for help and shield our true issues because we don't desire to be vulnerable. We don't want to be judged.

I've been asking if dysfunction has become a healthy medium for life. I feel shackled most times to some of my dysfunction, like a hoarder keeping dead weight with no release. How do we relearn what we've become accustomed to, and how do we try and become better and do things in a healthier manner? First, we must be willing to break out of the old ways and step into the new. Then, we must understand that we can't get stuck in our issues and make excuses on why not to change. Most, people don't know that their way isn't right. The fact is that we were all raised different, taught differently and did things differently. So, based on your upbringing it can be tough to understand the way others showcase their background. So, it's hard to change anyone else, but changing yourself can be very tough as well. When you begin to look at the person you've become - from your eating habits, to people you befriend, to addictions; down to how we treat people it says a lot about you individually. Learning to live life in a healthier way takes time and effort. Habits that you've formed for years become your way of life But, it's well worth the effort. Some of us need help and are too prideful to admit that we have issues. Whether they are from generational causes or down to the fact that so many of us were raised missing some major component in our lives. These issues affect us because we never sat down to even face the fact that we may have a problem. These issues cause damage to us and the people who are around us at times., but we sweep them under the rug and act as if we aren't affected. There is a bomb waiting to explode, and we don't even realize it. It begins to hinder relationships and bonds, and we usually think it's normal activity. Reminisce on how you were raised, and you will see how it has affected your life and actions. Sometimes, we can't blame our parents because when we look at what they were taught and how they were raised, realize that they gave us what they also had. It usually dates back several generations before us, and there is a lot of unhealthy "Stuff" there. The prior generational issues can't be changed but you can break the cycle for you and your future generations. Help Me! I need to relearn to live a healthy life.

Chapter 6

K issing cousins may be an uncomfortable topic, but were here for truth. Some may think who kisses their cousin. And others may wonder what is she about to say now? First make a note that if you've ever been touched by a family member or someone who is like family this chapter is for you. Yes, this chapter is meant to encourage us to be real and address more complex issues.

Here we grow! Some   people are very sexual and promiscuous, and have chalked it up to the fact they like sex. For some this may be true but for others it could be some underline issues behind the desire for sex. In this chapter kissing cousin refers to individuals who have been touched by an authority figure in their lives. Mom, dad, cousin, sister, brother, teacher and so on. In the African American community so many of us were introduced to sex at an early age. We knew the word 'Hunch or Hump oh too well. Many have participated in it, and the sad part is that it was mostly with a family member.

I've come to notice through speaking with "kissing cousin's victims" similar issues; such as addiction to alcoholism, eating and sleeping disorders, sexual disfunction, trust issues of the opposite sex, prostitution, promiscuity just to name a few. From an early age you were introduced to an act that should be shared between two people who are in love, not LUST, but love. Sex is meant for married couples, and the Bible also agrees with this in **Hebrews 13:4** and **1 Corinthians 7:9**. Now, I'm not here to blast you, because I'll be the first to say that I didn't wait until marriage. I was a mother as a teenager for those who don't know. Now, let's think about this? As a young child, you're being fondled and caressed and in some cases sexually penetrated–with a member of your family or someone close. Don't be ashamed you're in good company, many if willing to admit it have been introduced to homosexual sex and heterosexual sex by close members of your family. People who you trusted and cared for. I know this may be graphic for many but will send the intended message. This is immoral, unhealthy and where many emotional problems arise. Some may notice parenting issues as an adult. Being overprotective, not wanting to parent at all, always trying to prevent it from happening to our children, so we don't allow them to really live free. Individuals who are victims may also notice the inability to leave situations as easy, even when the signs and the chances are there. The mindset to stay and endure pain is more common after becoming a victim.

I'm speaking about it because I've experienced it from both male and female family members. And for many it may not have hit you that many of your underlined issues came from sexual interaction as a child with a love one. Let me help someone who is holding onto sick sexual introductions and wondering where this sexual demon came from. Or why you battle or are confused on if you desire sex from a man or woman. Or if you feel as women you can't trust men. Or as men they seek many sex partners. Many also associate sex with love, meaning if we have sex then the person loves us. I'm speaking on it, so your children and grandchildren won't be hurt in this manner. Were so free when it comes to family and close friends and even people we date. We don't always know what demons people suffer from. Most often we never tell about this part of our lives we shield it to protect our family unit. We don't want people we love hurt but this type information. I know what it can do to your sexual desires. I was introduced to the touch of a male and female at a very young age. Remember that we are discussing imprints on our lives. I decided to like the touch of both males and females for a period. Although many will be stunned by this or even embarrassed don't be. Being able to be honest with yourself is a step to healing and facing the pain. As I got older I knew it was the beginning of sexual demons. And often I recognize like spirits or those who have also suffered being abused sexually.

It can become a traumatic sexual disaster for you if never faced. Not saying you can't go on and live a normal life, I'm stating that you just may have some issues doing so. What we consider to be normal in many instances turn us into damaged goods. The damage goods are placed on the shelf as normal goods. How can I be a normal person when my experience of sexual violation was never discussed, and I was never counseled, and it was never dealt with as if it didn't happen? I grew up seeking sex as the answer to many issues. I allowed sex to be payment for love, hurt and pain in so many cases. I for sure have stayed past my expiration date with many men because of sex.

The foundation to anything must be solid, and when it's not it can crumble. Am I blaming anyone for desiring both male and female relationships in the past? Nope, but I'm trying to help people get healed. I've discussed with adults who told me that they had been touched by an aunt, cousin, uncle, brother or sister the hurt or issues it has caused. Most said the same thing they never would discuss it. Both men and women alike have violated children, and in some situations, they get caught and it is swept under the rug. It becomes an issue never to be discussed and addressed. This method of sweeping the case under the rug, in turn creates a barrier that says it's okay and normal and we may continue such behavior in our adult life and often in secret.

Now, we might have had reason to wonder why another person behaves sexually as they do. Why does he or she have so many sex partners. So much stems from the root of a situation that took place during our youthful years. Stop judging people because you will never know people's deep secrets. So many people have been kissed by their cousin maybe not literally but in retrospect. No matter who it was, if a family member or close friend has touched you in any way, it wasn't right, but you were not in any way wrong.

Now, should you go and seek professional help? I will say yes because you are still hurt and damaged by the act of sex that was introduced in a manner far from healthy. You're now trying to function as an adult and desiring a healthy relationship or marriage and can't understand this demon that has you bound. Causing desires and relationships that maybe if addressed you'd run from. Sexual demons and soul ties are real. Let's not pretend that this is okay. This is what causes us to shelter our children dramatically. Don't allow your childhood sexual experiences to linger and become more of a burden that has you bound. I'm not saying that you must expose the person who violated you to the world, but I would like to see you heal from the trauma, move on and live a healthy life. You deserve the HELP you need to be normal and enjoy love and sex the proper way. Things that hurt you badly need to be pulled out, plucked from the root and thrown away. Not just that, we must forgive others who didn't apologize to us most times. Not for their sake, but for the sake of a healthy life. Don't get me wrong. Sex is a wonderful thing if done in the right way. You might wonder why people seek sex and misuse it like they do, if you check their history, you may see evidence where a demon's stem took root. Many people were sexually abused by someone they knew, and still deal within family roles to this day. Not healthy but has become function in dysfunctional situation. This could be to keep from hurting others they love. Prevent this type of activity and live healthy sexual lives.

Chapter 7

W hen you think about love and your heart what is your thought? After many years of experience, I've discovered everyone's perception of love is different. Love is more than the shape we draw and emojis we send. And based on individual experiences we will see everyone's heart is different. My answer may not be same as yours and that's to be understood. Some common knowledge we all know is the heart the primary organ that keeps us functioning day after day. It pumps daily to push blood through our entire body. It has such a profound responsibility. But conversely, it's been cruel, misleading, and hurtful at times. I've asked on many occasions "Can I just get a new one, or borrow hers or his". My heart has carried me down some dark roads. My heart has overpowered my mind on many occasions. I have major love for people and their wellbeing. I can honestly say maybe its genetics; my family is the same way. But, I've seen that a big hurt can bring big hurt. This is the part of me that has been so big and so open to people, it has also led me down the path of hurt and destruction. It plays a big part in my decisions and my actions. Through time it has also become a hard heart. One that has needed some heart surgery. Not literally but some healing had to take place with it. When you have a big heart, people realize it and can at time it attracts people who don't have your best interest at hand. One day when speaking to my dad he said when you date again date the person who has a heart/love for you verses the person you have a heart for or love.

The problem is many of us suffer from just knowing the word love, but we have no clue of what it is. So, let me give my definition to me love is the most powerful feeling we can experience. The crazy thing is, that people only know how to use the word, but unaware of how to show it or give it back. Were clueless we associate love with so much that has nothing to do with it. We are confused and relate it to items, and sayings and emojis and its far from it.

It is so important to know and learn what the true meaning of words, not to just say them, but to apply them to our lives as well. Love comes in many definition and many of us don't know this, so we don't apply them properly. Love isn't the same in all situations. A love for family and for a spouse can be different. There are seven states of Love that you should learn and become more aware of to apply them properly.

Philautia: the love of the self (negative or positive)
Eros: sexual, passionate or romantic love.
Storge: is affectionate love, this love is the love you have for a family member.
Phileo: the friendship love or brotherly love.
Agape: this is the unconditional love, selfless love or charity. This is an act of the will to love.
Ludus: The gameplaying type of love, Lies, flirting and uncommitted type of love. Strange but yes.
Mania: obsessive or possessive, jealous and extreme deep love.
Pragma: long standing love. The love in a married couple.

Now that you can visually see what the types of love are you can now better understand how the play a role in your life and how to apply them. I'm not sure if it's something I've suffered or is it just the love I have that make me desire to give so much love to others. The tough part is that the love I give is rarely reciprocated in the manner that I expect. Everyone's heart isn't the same. We don't see or feel the same, and we can't force anyone's heart to love, beat or function as ours does. We must understand that with every heart comes many parts that we may not understand. – There is so much that people will never share that has made their heart hard to love. We know that we all have a heart, but no two hearts are the same no matter what. They may be compatible but not the same. I've had to learn some of the lessons of life the hard way. In my opinion, this is the perfect way because it's learned through experience. I don't feel anyone can teach us love, I feel it's learned through the lessons of life.

My experiences have taught me to have a severe, hardened heart. I began to expect love in so many different shapes and forms that I started to ask if exist. I read the Bible, and I desired the love that God speaks of. This is the agape love listed above. Many of us don't know this type of love. Let's look at the kind of love God has. We love our children and we can say we will do anything for them even die for them. One day I thought if someone asked to shoot me or my child do I have that type love for them. It's a thought. We all say yes. But, if it took place and were in this situation what would we say?

I've given my heart to people who used it, broke and stepped on it. I started to look back and dissected my life. I looked at my dad for instance. I know he loves me and I will never question his love for me. But I must be honest, he never said "I love you growing up". One day, when I spoke with him as I was older, and we were faced with a tough situation he started saying it. He said he never experienced hearing I love you when growing up. This was a revelation that the cycle he was raised in affected me too. We can't select our family like we select our friends. No wonder he loved me through his actions. He may have felt I didn't need to hear him say I love you. Or that it would ever affect me. I now seek and give love through my actions by providing and ensuring that things are in the right order.

So many of us lack love for ourselves therefore we have a tough time giving love to anyone else. How can you possibly not love who God created you to be? The lack of love to me is from insecurities and issues that are within you. To try and love a person when you've not found a passion to really love who you are can be a tough job. When you become whole enough to give yourself love then to baby you are on your way. It makes it easier to reciprocate love to others.

I think that what we expose our hearts to is very important. Now, that I'm a mother myself the way I raise my kids is a real example of how I was raised. I'm a very tough and stern parent, not often the loving mom that I've seen portrayed on TV or in some families. This could be the fact that I have three boys or the fact this is how love was shown to me growing up. We are products our environment and how we were raised. I feel that I've become what I saw while growing up. I can change if I'm taught or desire a change. But, how often do we initiate re-learning the things that we need to? I'm a product of how I was raised. So, love to me may not be the display that you received. And with this we must be careful on how we show love. The definitions or the examples may or may not be the same. This is something you must discuss with your mate or friends. Help others to understand your heart and how you love. It helps people better understand how you are and how you apply love in your life. Help Me I need Love.

Chapter 8

"Oh yes, it's true" as the Famous T.T. would state. Everybody won't like you, won't show concern for you, won't support you, and for sure won't be your cup of TEA. Hello, it's true. Guess what, that's OKAY. You don't have to please everyone, hang out with everyone, or expect support and love from everyone, because everyone can't see the greatness that lies in you. Stop wasting your precious time of convincing people of who you are and why you're great. I use to be so consumed with how other people felt about me, being liked, and how people talked bad about me. What really use to get me is the fact that a lot of it was not true. We all know I didn't write this book to waste your time or my time, so I won't act like I haven't done some ole savage mess in my day. But, at least give me my mess and keep what you weren't sure of. But, with age you'll see the more they talk the more they see you making moves.

One thing nobody can do is make me feel I'm not who I am. I've suffered some rough spots in life that forced me to see me for me. Even with all I've done, with all my faults I still am who I am. And I love her. See the issues is as I stated above too many people lack the love they need for themselves. They are not whole, so people determine who they are. Always seeking others to justify your greatness. When you are healed from "Peopleism" makes life a little easier to function. We know that social media has made it easier for people to lift you up and tear you down. This platform allows people to be frauds and pretend when they really aren't who they post to be. But, it allows love some people lack to be shown for people to feel accomplished when otherwise they never would.

You are your own person and you must be true to yourself. When you start trying to fit in and be liked by everyone you end up hurting you. Everyone isn't meant to even be in your presence, because everyone wasn't created to fit your life. One of the biggest dream killers is "What will people think, say or feel" my answer is who cares. Be the best you can be whether they love it or not.

People are so miserable with themselves nowadays, that they only know to make everyone they interact with the same way. Misery will show from miles away. If they feel the need to talk about everyone. No matter what the situation they feel need to negative. I've learned that misery is like a virus it spreads. Miserable people are everywhere on our jobs, in our families, at church and the work overtime to spread their toxic lives into others. Watch how you change when certain negative Nancy's or negative Ned's show up. The enemy is aware of this, notice after prayer ow when you're in your best mood something just shows up to through you off. Begin to recognize and combat the enemy when he attacks. See its easy to manage issues when you recognize them. Stop falling for the same mess from the devil.

I feel that social media plays a significant role in the misery of people. Why, because they see so many people putting on like life is grand and they have nothing going on. Social media has allowed so many people the ability to be who they never would without it. People are in secret coemption with social media post that 9 times out of 10 aren't even factual. So many people are trying to be liked and loved by folks who don't even like or love themselves. One thing about maturity is the fact that you when you mature you can stand on your own two feet. Without justification from the world. We will never outgrow chatter from other people, it's just how life is.

You don't have to fit in, dress like everyone, or go wherever they go, just be yourself. So many people have an ID theft issue in their lives, because they have stolen someone else's identity, claimed it to be theirs, and they are okay with it. Fake is for sure the new reality and we all know that it's easier to fit into the world than it is for us to stand out and be alone. So, many people are just existing, buying the same shoes, wearing the same clothes, buying the same cars, and trying to keep up with each other. We never seem to be satisfied. We are always trying to compete or gain more than others.

I remember when I was trying to be liked by so everyone, I lived a fake life and I had issues with the way God wanted me to live my life. I wanted to fit in and needed the approval of people who never got to even know me. In fact, I saw so much fake love because I've always trying to be approved. So, I began to attract takers or leaches. I gave so much of me trying to be liked and popular. As I looked back today, I realize that I was in dire need of self-discovery. Some people would never admit this truth, but I'm real with myself and others need to be real with themselves too. You've hung out with people who never meant you any good and you knew it. We hung with people who wanted us to do well but not better than them. Many are suffering in forced relationships due to a need to be validated by someone else to feel relevant. Many people are living fake lives with no intent of being real. The moment you become true to yourself, you won't allow yourself to settle for fake friends and counterfeits. You'll be strong enough to stand alone if you can't stand with strong accountable partners. Even exercise caution regarding those you ride along with these days. Some people desire other people's lifestyles and they are jealous and full of envy. You never know what people's real intentions are. One of the biggest lessons of my life came from a friend. I learned quickly, and without any second of doubt, evicted, cut off and deleted her. People can only act for so long before the script runs out and they begin to show their true colors and intentions. Don't ever be a fool and ignore the signs. Many people admire the lifestyle of their friends because they are not content with their own. It's hard to walk in someone else shoes, believe me, I tried it until I found my lane and owned it. My walk is a tad easier to walk.

Self-discovery took time and desire, it became a burden for me to get to know myself other than who I was to others. I wanted to gain my identity after so many failed attempts at being like others; being faker than a three-dollar bill and asking why there was a need for this. The need for relationships is paramount to people nowadays. We are social creatures and we desire to be loved even if it's not real. Sad, but it's true that we desire to be loved by any means and we want to fit in and be recognized. I'll leave you with this thought. Too often, we allow people to stay way past their expiration in our lives. We must decide to uncover and dissect the true us and those who surround us. People have to be able to accept you for you and you have to require it. We all can use some grow up time. We need this for a healthy life. We can't live forever trying to be liked, loved and fit in. We must decide to be the best we can be and those who are supposed to be a part of the journey genuinely will be people who are honest, those who motivate us, and love us for who we are. Those who will correct us in love and truth and celebrate us when we rise and help us when we're down. A genuine person who is meant for you will help you row your boat in the direction you are going, and will not put holes in it and wait for the boat to fill up and sink. Know who is meant for you and who is against you. Help Me! I need to know whose riding and who is just waiting for my downfall.

Chapter 9

Most people dread the difficult, challenging conversation. This includes conversations in which we must deliver unpleasant news, discuss a delicate subject, or talk about something that needs to change or has gone wrong. In life, we avoid communication of the such. Social media, text messages, and messaging services have become our new way of communicating. I realized recently when something was done that hurt me, that I often run from talking about hurtful situations, I tend to just avoid the situation or person altogether. I would be willing to throw them away and forget that they exist, to keep from speaking on it. Or either ignore it until I was at a level of such anger that I would explode and say whatever came to mind hurtful, disrespectful or cruel this is my communication method.

The thing is I know this is not right and I've done it for so long I realize this how I've learned to handle conversations. During a recent conversation with my mentor, she said: "This isn't adult behavior in her sweetest voice." I stopped, looked and evaluated our conversation and although at times we know what's right we need to hear it. Yes, she was right and knew that, but at times the truth is hard to accept. I know that I need to make some adjustments. I know I must re-learn how to communicate properly even with tough conversations. My questions became how did my method of communication get here? I'm an adult and I run from conversations that may not have a happy ending. I began to self-evaluate why this had become a normal habit. Why do I avoid the conversations that aren't simple? And it hit me. Because we love what's simple, easy and good. I don't want anyone angry at me over even what may be hurting me. To think about a harsh response isn't always easy. We don't like tough, adverse and challenging situations. But, how can we grow and know what the intentions, thoughts, or reasons behind a person's actions are if we never actually discuss it? How can someone know they hurt you or how they made you uncomfortable if a conversation isn't had? I thought wow, how many relationships have been aborted due to non-communication? Due to not being honest and addressing issues when they happen.

It's clear to me and I now see that people don't think alike. We weren't raised alike, and we don't always understand each other. I realized that some people weren't exposed to or taught certain things and will never be able to see things the way I do if we don't discuss. I'll be the first to admit that I'm stuck in my ways. But, I'll be the first also to confess that I'm ready for growth and I pray to be teachable each day. What if I had stopped to share my thoughts and express my feelings, what if I had sat down to see why the other person's actions were as they were? I've been so use to running when the going gets tough, that I sometimes feel I missed out on some great relationships. The word communication means *the imparting or exchanging of information or news to get a clear understanding.* How can we get a clear understanding if we don't communicate? I feel that's why we run to text and messaging services nowadays to speak because it allows us to hide our expressions, tears and emotions. It gives us more freedom to say what we would never usually say in a direct conversation. It allows us to hide our true concerns from the other person because we can't see through a message as we could if the person was in front of us. Right now, I diligently try to have tough conversations no matter what. This is not just for me but for those who matter to me. I don't want to lose someone because we didn't converse on an issue that needed only a simple conversation.

We seek to be in healthy relationships if we can't speak on what affects us in positive and adverse situations. Don't run from what needs to be addressed. So often our thoughts are the same with those of others, and because we have a preconception of their intentions and thoughts. Communication can bring clarity and prevent misunderstandings if we apply the ability to just converse. Communication rules the nation. I won't say every conversation will be easy but if a conversation needs to be had its necessary.

We must also use wisdom and think before we speak. We can't take words back once we utter them. The tongue is a powerful weapon, and it's often used for more harm than good. We can't rewind words that we've spoken that may have hurt and even shatter another person. People don't want to be vulnerable about what they feel, so we can often try and avoid saying what needs to be said. We don't always want to share deep thoughts, so we avoid speaking. We don't always know how or what to say. And the best thing for situations when you lack words is not speak until you have what to say. Angry situations can cause us to spit out words that we don't always mean and can't take back. and kind while talking, everything can be conveyed in a manner such as to show respect for another person.

I've said some mean and hurtful things to people in my day. I've intentionally said things to damage and cause harm through words. When speaking in anger it's a deadly weapon towards another person. I've said things that I don't even want to repeat. One thing I know is I'm not perfect, and I seek forgiveness for some of my ways and actions. I know that I can come up with the meanest words in situations to prevent people from hurting me. I know my conversations sometimes came from dark places that contain jealousy, malice, anger and hurt. I know that even when you are truthful, you can still look back and think that you may have revealed too much. Many of us avoid honesty and the dirty little secrets that we have in our life safe. I always knew that lying to others is one thing but lying to thyself is something else.

Communication is so essential or is it? We can't make it a habit of acting as if talking to a person isn't essential especially if you care for them.

Every conversation won't hold the same weight. We get mad and we often make it a habit to go and speak to others about situations that we should be speaking to the offender about. We make subliminal post on social media that hint we are offended or upset to release frustration. Does this make you a coward for being big enough to speak on an issue that you can't take to the person. Most issues come from the lack of communication and misunderstanding. We make assumptions and have beef at times and the offender is clueless they have even offended. The horrible part is that we spread the issues before we try and cure it.

Some may not agree but the importance of communication can also depend upon the relationship or the situation. If you don't have a very strong relationship with a person, then why waste time on explaining yourself or battling. I know we are in a time where we feel we must explain ourselves when we have been criticized or talked about. Often, we speak when we shouldn't and are quiet when we should speak. Prioritizing when and who to speak to and how is important and a must for your sanity and your growth. Holding onto issues will cause them to fester.

Before I end, I have a memory that I must share. I remember being so hurt, having so much anger and avoiding a conversation with someone close to me I said: "If you die, I won't come to your funeral." The person died a few weeks later, and I never got the chance to take those words back. I know this came from a place of hurt. From a situation that was unresolved between the two us. I never will be able to take the words back and I really don't want to think I allowed hurt to cause me to cause harm to a person in my dark time. I know this hurt the individual because they revealed the conversation with someone close to me later but never to me. Assuming we had discussed the issue and avoided hurtful words, we could have understood one another from each other perspective. I can't change the words I spoke, but I learned from them. One thing for sure is that I will always try to avoid words of this nature or even if I fall Ill try to resolve them. My words soon became my reality. I'm working on myself even to this day. Today, I say HELP ME! I want to learn to communicate in tough situations properly.

Chapter 10

∞

R ecently, I realized that forgiveness isn't for the other person, but for me. What does this mean and why the heck is it so important?

Forgiveness: *to stop feeling anger toward (someone who has done something wrong): to stop blaming (someone): to stop feeling anger about (something): to* **forgive** *someone for (something wrong): to stop requiring payment of (money that is owed).*

The meaning is clear, so let me begin by saying that forgiveness doesn't always have to be for someone else, sometimes we must forgive ourselves. Sometimes, we must let go of the pain that we have caused ourselves, the things we've allowed, the situations we created and so on and so forth. So many conversations I've had with people have taught me the significance of forgiveness. I woke up one day facing the reality that I had a lot of anger towards myself that needed to be forgiven. I take my time now to dissect and analyze myself better and I see flaws, scars, hurt and what I've mask that others will never see. I know that some of the blame that I carry needs to be forgiven and thrown into the same sea of forgetfulness that Jesus pitches them into. But, why is this an arduous task? Why do we carry issues for so long, why do we drag ourselves through long drawn out journeys? It became clear to me that I needed to be more like Jesus and I for one sincerely needed to know Him better to do so. But if I don't know what the Bible says about forgiveness how can I know the instructions from the Lord. So, let's consider it together. These three verses speak of forgiveness, and I took note of them as follows:

"Get rid of all bitterness, passion, and anger. No more shouting or insults, no more hateful feelings of any sort. Instead, be kind and tender-hearted to one another, and forgive one another, as God has forgiven you through Christ." **(Ephesians 4:31-32)**

"If you forgive others the wrongs they have done to you, your Father in heaven will also forgive you. But if you do not forgive others, then your Father will not forgive the wrongs you have done." **(Matthew 6:14-15)**

"So, if you are about to offer your gift to God at the altar and there you remember that your brother has something against you, leave your gift there in front of the altar, go at once and make peace with your brother, and then come back and offer your gift to God." **(Matthew 5:23-24)**

It's clear that I'm obligated to forgive others for hurting me and leaving more scars on my life, no matter how I feel about it. I've learned that the best way to forgive is to just do it. Just not be held hostage by another person's strife. If I'm being held hostage by their actions, I'm no better than them. Ouch, that hurt!

The fact that I always need to be forgive because the words states that I must forgive to be forgiven. I get it. But, I know it's not that easy. Some folks have done some horrible things to me in my day. Does this allow me not to forgive, Of course not? We have so much life to live, so being bound by the past hurt and foolishness of others isn't worth it. At times, people do things carelessly, and they later realize their actions were painful and harmful to the other person. Karma is a well-known word that we throw it around like a ball daily. Karma is for sure a two-way street. It doesn't only apply to those who have hurt us, but it applies to you and me as well. We all have done so messed up stuff to others. The same forgiveness that we seek is set for us to give also. We can hurt people, that's our choice, but we must know that we reap what we sow, good or bad. No matter how justified it is we must pay for it. What I often think of is God isn't going to ask me what you did to me, but what

I did and how I reacted to you. That is or should be enough to guide you. You are responsible for you own actions.

There are some people that we need to forgive, and we don't even realize they have hurt us or caused us pain. We must sit, think, and pray for God to reveal who has caused us pain that we may not recognize. We need to know each person who has hurt us and begin the process of growth in our hearts to forgive. I'm not saying you must be friends, hang out, or even kiss and make up with everyone that has hurt you. But, I'm advising you to be free from the hurt others have inflicted. In some cases, you may start afresh with someone who has hurt you in the past, but that's a choice you must pray about to know the best decision to take. Some people grow and truly realize they messed up and may never cause any more harm. Everyone can't be thrown to the wolves they are a part of your story. In some instances, God uses who will get our attention. Everyone won't influence our heart like others.

I feel a person must forgive every person who has hurt them big or small. Start a forgiveness list, pray and ask God who has hurt you. He will begin to reveal those from child hood on up to adult hood. A person may just have had some scars from their childhood that they never knew could become an issue until they start on their forgiveness list. As I stated above, some issues are hidden deep down, and they must be revealed to you. The issues that you had in a place and that you weren't even aware of. So, I'm asking you to say HELP! Who do I need to forgive and why? Also, take me as far back as possible. I found out that writing helps me to see things that I didn't know or realize. Help Me I must forgive.

Chapter 11

S ex means different things to different people. Sexuality is so influential now days. It's all over television, social media and in our face daily. Some people really haven't found the true meaning of it yet. Above all, it is a healthy and a very natural activity. It is something most people enjoy and find meaningful even if they create meaning in diverse ways. Whether you're straight, lesbian, gay, bisexual, or questioning what your preference is, you have the right to decide what your definition is to you.

Nowadays, sex is so easy to get. Heck! There are online sites promoting sex with ads and people who are just looking for an enjoyable time. You ride down the street, and people are on corners selling sex. Sex is the new hip thing in our society and don't get me wrong now. I'm not speaking bad about sex. I'm not ashamed to help someone out today. Often sex is a topic we run from speaking on publicly. We don't want to offend, and Lord knows we don't want everyone knowing were having sex if not married. I believe therefore when I got pregnant it was so tough to discuss. I'm sure some people were minding my business and saying things like. "I know she is having sex" I know that dude hitting that" "She aint telling she is having sex on them lives." Did I hit the nail on the head? One thing you'll never get from me is bashing anyone's choices. This is because God doesn't even do that he is a freewill kind of God. He doesn't force anything on anyone. But, get this find anytime I've said I wasn't getting my sex on and we can discuss it.

I speak real life when it comes to any conference, live or speaking engagement. I'm not a motivational speaker I'm a truth speaker and sometime that doesn't motivate anyone. I want to be transparent, so you understand me and feel that I've been there too. Sometimes people need the real you, not the dressed up, made up, fake you. But, your struggles, your brokenness and masked like. So, yes to Jesus assistants Mel fornicates and Jesus will deal with me there. Thanks for your help.

I've experienced my fair share of sex in my life. Now don't go trying to count a number for fair share and telling people you know the number. I realized that some of my sexcapades were because of some very uncomfortable childhood experiences, peer pressure, loneliness and just desire to feel wanted. I can also equate some to messed up relationships, some games I was playing and habit. Sex has been an outlet when going through. To be honest I don't need sex, I'm no addict and I can for sure go extended periods without it. You must be careful of who you dibble with in bed for more reason than a baby and STD's. I'll say that once I began to have sex, I would prefer to be with the same person for as long as possible. Because I've heard people want to speak on the fact on being a whore if you had a lot of partners. So, I tried to make my sex life the best it could be, so the men would stay around. You know like put on for my sex partner, he needs to be here a while. I know there are people who like to bed hop that's not my preference. After hearing a few times from men that sex with me was a pleasant experience that was like calling me beautiful. And it was on from there. Sex was a manipulation tactic to stay with a man. I figured I would try and use sex as a weapon and to my advantage. Even if I knew a person was far from what I needed Id keep them around if we'd had sex. We become habitual abusers of sex just to have something to do. Sad, but its true now women utilize sex as leverage and have many sex partners just as men do. This use to be unheard of. Oh, how times have changed.

So many people don't understand that sex means more than an orgasm. It's supposed to be a great, magical, fulfilling experience between two people who are married. Sighs, yes, we are supposed to be married. Sex outside out marriage can bring soul ties. There is no right or wrong way no time limit or even rule to it. It's what two people feel is best for them. I think Monica had people thinking getting down on the first night was a no go for a minute. Many don't know what all sex involves. How it can affect two people and what connections it can bring between them. Well, let's learn a few things; When we have a sex with an individual male or female, our brains produce what's called dopamine, the same chemical that pushes a gambler, the chemical that triggers drug user to use, and your food addiction. Dopamine is the trigger for your brain as well. The thing about our bodies is its don't care what your drug of choice is, dopamine will be produced, and it will control us. Your drug of choice may not be the same as my drug but we all have the same chemical reaction. So, with sex it kicks in and when the dopamine can make us think we are in love and we need more of a person when really the chemical is handling us as it does a drug user.

The problem is most of haven't put the standard to be married so its not popular. Fornication has been popular for a long time. But, because we are a follower when we see popular people showing marriage as a wonderful thing this now becomes "Goals" and then we want it. But, if marriage was pushed more then more would desire it. Sex is sold to us mentally on so many levels. Our world suffocates us with sexual acts that causes it to be popular. A video popped up on one of the social media outlets of women in a line giving men head in a club setting like a competition. This is what we are showing our kids. Twerk videos are normal. Sex sells whether were buying or not it's selling to someone.

Some of my longest relationships lasted with quick sex. So, the conversation if having sex, the first night matters or not one to be discussed. Well, if you have sex with someone in 2 months and still know no more about them than the first night what's the difference? It's a preference thing. I don't know if the test drive before you buy rule is in affect for sexual encounters, but for me some of my longest relationships came from first nighters. I was even made a wife from one and have beautiful children. So, the world can't dictate your story.

We must evaluate our decisions on the partners we select and why? We must understand that every person we sleep with can leave an impression on us. Every person we feel is good enough to share our love through sex should be of quality. People have so many issues that are hidden you never know what they come with honestly. People desiring to spread aids and viruses for fun. STD's are at an all-time high. I saw a picture that showed an example of how many partners you have based on how many sex partners you've had. It showed that once you sleep with one person you've now slept with every person they've been with and so on. Not to mention soul ties they are like a tangled web. If you've had sexual encounters outside of marriage, consensual or forced, there is most like a 1 soul tie connected. If it's not dealt with it will forever hold onto you with bombarding your thoughts, feelings and even actions. I mention forced sex because, although we don't enjoy sexual abuse, our brains still produce dopamine reactions and we are still tied to the offender.

I think now days sex is just a thing to do or a time passer. I heard an artist state that once he has an orgasm he comes back to his senses meaning his sex high dies when dopamine stops kicking in. Everybody is just having sex, absolutely no feelings involved and no concern for one another. In some cases, not even knowing one another. Meaning knowing more than a name of a person. We don't even have to know each other, no background, and no knowledge of each other and boom bam; the deal is done.

Women get pregnant and feel a man is forever attached to them. A baby *isn't* going to keep a man, or make him desire to do right by your child. Therefore, we must be careful who we decide to sex and procreate with, not only women but men as well. Every woman isn't on the right path just like every man isn't. There are people out here in the world who are so damaged they seek to only have sex and that's it.

Take note that I'm far from a woman basher, but being a woman I know that we tend to manipulate and misuse men with sex. It seems that the women who get the best men are the women who can be a damaging factor. There are some amazing men in the world who only seek to be a good mate. Men just like women have major damage. They've been hurt and abused, and they have emotions and they react as well. Some men are getting the short end of the stick due to broken women and who they selected to have sex with. Men tend to be less confrontational and us women know this. We use it to our advantage.

I know many great men who have had sex and it made a baby. There are women who feel they can manipulate things to keep a man by having a baby with them. I know many women who seek a baby for child support and leverage. Yes, I said leverage to try and control the man's life. Let's not leave out those women who won't allow the man to see the baby if they aren't together, the ones who won't allow the baby to be around anyone else and those who always want to force the dad to their house to see the child, provide. Get over it people, hit the cup and get out when you see the signs. Use protection and know who you are sleeping with, just because a person offers good sex, head, or looks good doesn't mean they are good for you or to procreate with. Please start studying your mate before you decide to have children.

Sex sells as we all know. Therefore, sex is so important nowadays. What else do we have to offer to one another? If we take away sexy bodies and money many people would have nothing to offer. We look at the features of a person and often their features don't equate to a quality mate for what they have to offer or give. It's becoming an epidemic now days to just sex and move on. Love is so hard to find, and we are accepting whatever is dished out. Sex is just something to do in our down time. Men fear commitment and women are afraid to set standards, so we seem to be a bit lost. Help Me why is sex so important?

Chapter 12

~~~~~~~~

R elationships are complex or at least we make them that way. They can be anything from a strong dealing with teens, on over to a very bonded friendship, an intense sexual experience you're having with the someone, or a marriage. These days, everyone's in a relationship or trying to be. A relationship is not just a boyfriend and girlfriend the definition of a relationship is:

noun

> 1. *the way in which two or more concepts, objects, or people are connected, or the state of being connected.*

Meaning a relationship is any ship that has a connection. This is your friends, co-workers and so on. We must just be sure that all our ships are flowing in the same direction we desire. We can't be unsure of the people who we allow to sail with us meaning unsure of the people we allow in our lives. I like to look at relationships like building blocks to a partnership. Relationships are those meaningful experiences you have with people that either die out or turn into something greater. Every relationship isn't replaceable. Everyone isn't meant to stay forever.

When it comes to relationships, there is no standard size or definition for them. Every relationship comes with its own set of rules and dialogue. A relationship is more than something we want—it's something we need to be our happiest, healthiest, most productive selves. But at home or work, supportive, fulfilling relationships don't come automatically. They take an investment in time and energy as well as communication and social skills that can be learned. When I speak on being learned meaning we must put work into them for them to grow and healthy.

We've all had some beautiful, romantic, futile emotional relationships that can either disappear as if they never existed, the ones that fall off with great intensity or the ones that form into something grand, more powerful and more purposeful. In relationship's I feel the saying "People are for a season and some are for a lifetime" is true amongst all relationship's.

I know that a common issue is that we often rush into relationships, without any knowledge of the person. Many of us are big on titles to make us feel its solidified. But, how can we feel we are ready for any relationship without the proper components to form one. You must know a person the real person. And many will argue it's a task to ever know who a person really is because it takes time. But, I also state that we need to know more than a first and last name to call it a true relationship.

Relationships should be a partnership. Let me say partnerships are however, are a different league. They are for individuals who have waded their way through some tough times, stuck through them and landed on something stronger than before. It's not what a person does when everything is at is best in when the going gets tough that you learn. It's important in my mind at the start of any relationship to have the tough discussions, like "How aware are you of your life issues and suppressed emotions, get to know people before you waste time that you can't get back. I know it may seem deep but aren't you worth not wasting time?

Therefore, so many marriages and relationships end. When the going gets tough some people get going. I'm not a supporter or being mistreated in anyway. But, I am one to fight for what I want. So, many relationships are ended due to cheating, abuse and just not giving two damns about the person who you're with. Relationships need love, nurturing, time, honesty, loyalty and respect. In them you must have boundaries and rules that two parties need to agree of compromise on. Its not just a giving situation it's a give and take situation. Meaning you must give some and take some. Its no way to have a perfect one, because no two people are perfect. But, you can have one that fits you.

One of my favorite relationships is the one that incorporates marriage. Although, marriage may not be a top choice of many due to the taunted reputation of them to meet your soul mate and start a lifelong relationship is a God ordained thing. Marriage is a legally or formally recognized union of two people as partners in a personal relationship (historically and in some jurisdictions specifically a union between a man and a woman). Now in this time it can be between any two people. This is the law in many states now. I can't tell a person who will make them happy. So, for whomever your soulmate is then this is for you to decide. But, in marriages it's supposed to be a relationship for two people to be committed, honest, supportive, loving and true. Now, I know, and you know that cheating is very popular. The era of the side chick or man is how many desire it to be. Marriages stock has gone down so far that people are willing to ruin marriages just to have what they want. Cheating is a key factor in marriages failed marriages. Brings me to ask can two people be faithful for a lifetime? Can we get through the next best thing approaching us selling us on how they can make our lives better? They can provide and make sure we are loved and cared for. See when it comes to a person wanting you they become the ultimate sales person. And with the issues that relationships carry this can be a crack in the door for another person. Giving up is easy and many people won't fight and have the mindset to leave and move on. In this age verses our grandparent's time relationships/marriages lasted forever. Now days we can barely stay committed to a job for a few months let a long a marriage or a stable relationship. We are spoiled, selfish and set in our ways. To change takes effort that most won't give. Therefore, failed relationships happen often. Look at the change of baes on social media, people change them openly without remorse. This shows rooted issues and the need for attention and approval. People are just our here damaging each other without care.

The instability of relationships comes from the opaqueness of feelings. Half the time and energy given in a relationship revolves around trying to figure out how the other person feels. Judging people based on our own feelings of how things should be. Partnerships aren't about feelings. The feelings have already been established and stabilized. Partnerships are about taking those feelings and proving them every day, meaning work is involved. If relationships are about finding the feelings, partnerships are about proving how real they are.

There are so many types of relationships, and if you decide to get into one they are important or should be. We often play with relationships, never taking them seriously, which is the problem with them lasting. In fact, relationships make the world go around. If we go into relationship with the mindset we will give them our all on all levels, we won't have as many dissipate. Relationships always look simple on the outside but are usually a mess and unstable on the inside. Relationships collapse because we don't invest the needed time to get to know the other person. If you don't have the patience and experience, there's just no holding it together. Partnerships take time, practice and complete trust. They are rarely formed because most people don't want to take the time to get there. Most individuals give up on the idea of a healthy relationship before they even attempt it.

Relationships change over time with issues and situations that arise. They are living, breathing arrangements that are constantly evolving and constantly need work. Relationship have many reasons that they change, and with anything change is scary. Yet, a good relationship can stand the test of time, and get better and better as we grow them if, you make your relationship a priority, and both partners are always growing and improving, and seeking to become better partners. Then like anything healthy

But, relationships can change in undesirable ways and bring you big surprises, especially if you haven't learned how to manage your relationships and how to be honest. It pays to learn how to deal with your relationships and to develop a tool box for each one individually. Relationships would be much easier, if only someone had given us a relationship manual. Chances are, though, you learned about relationships like the rest of us did. . through trial and error. Well, it's never too late. Now you can have that manual. Yes, you can teach an old dog new tricks if you're willing to. Help I need to know how to handle a relationship.

Chapter 13

A s I began the research to know what a friend was I saw that the Japanese have a term, *kenzoku,* which translated means "family." The connotation suggests a bond between people who've made a similar commitment and who could share a similar destiny. It implies the presence of the deepest connection of a friend.

Many of us have people in our lives we feel the bond described by the word kenzoku. They may be family members, a mother, a brother, a daughter, a cousin. Or a friend from school or a person you met in passing. Time and distance do nothing to diminish the bond we have with these kinds of friends. Often, we give the title when it's not deserved. I feel society embeds in us the title friend verses associate from childhood and we begin the cycle of calling everyone we meet a friend.

I must ask how and why do we form the bond encapsulated by the word kenzoku. We discover the importance of friends in tough times and when with time itself. The closer we look for the answer of who is a friend the more elusive it becomes. It may not in fact be possible to know, but the characteristics that define a *kenzoku* relationship most certainly are.

The urban dictionary states true friendship is not when you go to school and hang around with someone just because you have no one else to occupy your time. It's not calling someone up when you're bored.

Friendship is when you love someone and genuinely want the best for them like you desire for yourself. A devoted friend is someone you can talk to about anything. A person you can truly trust and depend on without question. They are someone who you don't have to talk to and pick back up where you left off. Someone you will go out of your way for. Someone you know you know you can lay your head on their shoulders at any given time. It's someone you can talk to about things to and disagree on and end up being closer for that disagreement.

In my older age I've had to discover what a friend truly is and how to be one. I haven't always been the best of a friend and really didn't desire to. I feel that at a stage in my life friendship was about who you were loyal to in their face. And, who had the most friends. It wasn't for years that I discovered that quality over quantity was important when it came to friends. Who can I depend on to pray for me, to tell me the truth and to be far from a "Yes Man". I didn't know the value of a friend until God placed some true Peters in my camp. Meaning some true ride or dies in my life. He placed some people in my life for a season at some points. I feel he was teaching what I needed and didn't need. I believe with some people he was trying to show me how I was through someone else. He was showing me that at some point you must be wise on who you call a friend. Its not who is true in your face but that person who you can depend on when you're down and out.

After many years of Russian roulette with friendships it taught me everyone won't be a friend for a lifetime. He allowed me to see the maturity in the sense of friendship. He showed me that everyone I send to your life isn't for friendship, some are for you to help come out of a familiar season. This makes discernment so key. Discernment is being able to know what role God has placed certain people in your life for. You can't take everyone in as a friend some people are to give you a reminder or something, some are to get you over the funk you're in. Some need to show you that trust is earned not given and loyalty is a must.

Everyone won't be in your life forever and that isn't a terrible thing. Some friends become enemies and that's all good too. Because in the word it states he will prepare a table before you enemies, which is verification you must have some in your life. I feel that often we get upset about people leaving our lives that we felt would be in our lives forever. Some bridges had to burn for some people not to be able to walk back in our lives. Some snakes had to hiss so we could stop calling them family and some backs had to turn for us to grow and move forward. The best part about some of my frenemies' I never would have let them go had they not crossed me. Therefore, the few I have now I value with all of me. Loyalty means a lot to me and being faithful to them is mandatory. They've been through some things and can relate to me when I go through. They get we must go through to grow through. My friends know that if I'm needed I'm there. We pray and encourage each other and a yes crew we are not. Each one of them bring something that God knows I need. We are not perfect, and we get what we give to one another is genuine. We aren't here to judge or spread each other's business. Were protective of one another. And lastly, we can worship, cry and pray for each other. This for me is friendship.

I know God cares for me through the people He's blessed me with. I know that he allowed some of the horrible people in my life to show me how horrible I was at a point as a friend. I can now say I am my sister's keeper. I have their back. I will pray for them in their time of need. No judgment no matter the situation. I am their vault with their secrets. I desire to see them be there very best. I think the above saying is true I've gained sisters in this season. I know that every day we won't always agree, and I love that. Because anything that seems perfect isn't what I want. Anyone who has not endured some hardship can go and anyone who feels the need to glorify other people hardship can't sit with me. I've gone through too much to be in the swing of others downfall. on others business and gossip and judge can go. Stable friendship is mandatory. And it must be for you. Today there may be some folks who you're questioning their position or role in your life use clear wisdom in the area of your life. One of my most profound revelations came as I stood before a judge to sentence me to prison. She was clear to me everyone isn't your friend and don't desire to see you do your best. Be careful on who you call friend and who you associate with. Because at one of the toughest times of my life I learned a valuable lesson on friendship. Be wise and selfish with you, your time and your space. Wisdom is for Help Us Lord we need to know what friendship really is.

Chapter 14

S o, let me share with you may life guide. Let's get some help here. The Bible is a very important book in my opinion. It may not have the same importance to everyone. To me it is my foundation to just about everything mankind will ever go through. It's for sure a teacher that guides through many tests. I'm not a Bible scholar and I can't quote a ton of Bible verses. But when I search it for a word, I always find it. I've made it a habit to get a word from the Bible daily and share it with a group of ladies to keep me in a place that requires the word. It shows many examples of how we should live. It's full of examples of what and how to do things. I'm pushing myself to become more knowledgeable of the Bible for many reasons, but my main aim is to learn how to get to know God as I desire to know everyone and thing else. How can I truly know Him if I don't study the book that reveals him? How can I honestly have this relationship I'm seeking without the bible? His reactions, His heart and how He loved and moved daily?

Nothing is new under the sun the Bible talked about sex, adultery, haters, liars, prostitutes, marriages, diseases and so much more. There are so many examples of how to overcome challenges. We can't get to know the Word if we don't study. Let me tell you a true short story. One day, I lost my debit card and I searched all over for it. It so happens that whenever life becomes horrible, I would pick up my Bible. I would read about relationship issues, money issues, work, struggles, family problems and men issues. I would get into the word heavily. So, I must have been in a bad mood when I mistakenly dropped my debit card in it. Eventually life must have picked up and I put my bible back down to collect dust. After a while life must have done what it does and caused me to need God, you know the whole put God on the shelf until things got rough deal. As I dusted my bible off and opened it up after months, my old faithful debit card popped out. It was like God was saying "Don't use Me baby girl, had you been faithful despite that man taking you through hell, you would have found this card months ago." If we were sincere, many of us would admit that we aren't as faithful as we should be in prayer and the Word. But, once life hits us hard, cancer strikes, mom or dad gets sick, legal issues spring up, money gets scarce, we then run to the Bible, fasting and prayer. That's a sign of using the God for personal gain. The Word is the same, and it's faithful regarding the God it speaks about. But are we faithful as we should be? So many of us are where we are today because we don't get it yet. The good thing about God is that He is not like you and me. He doesn't run off and forget us, He doesn't stop listening, He doesn't bash us and hate or even throw anything in our faces. He is the same God no matter how bad we are to Him. His word shows this when we take some time to pick it up and see who He is, and how He truly does things.

Some may have to study a little harder like in school to know the word like others. But, every can build their own personal relationship with God. Keep trying to learn the word and apply verses that help you in your current situations.   It's a verse for every situation. Read it with an open mind and open heart as often as possible. So many people are afraid that if the begin to read the bible they must make this drastic leap of change. Many are so broken from churches, pastors and leaders who have misused and mislead them. That now they have no desire to have a relationship with God. So many of us have witnessed the leaders that cover us do things that were less than perfect. Many have built us up and broken us down and left us high and dry. Therefore, so many people are running from the word and God. When you select a place of worship you seek to be led by truth and someone who is honestly seeking God and leading you towards God. There are so many leaders that look like wolves in sheep clothing that people feel they don't need assistance taking themselves to hell. Leaders are held to a different standard, and although were all human and all fall short and we have no space to judge. That has nothing to do with the affects a leader can cause on us in a bad way. Most people put a ton of stock in their leader and like any relationship when we feel betrayed we usually don't stick around. So, this usually doesn't just cause us to leave a church but puts distance and hinderances between us and God as well. Due to this person being a representation of the God they speak of day after day week after week when they misrepresent if affects the people they lead.

God doesn't call you to be perfect or holier than thy person. Nope, not true at all. It's the foundation to a solid foundation with God. It contains pure truth about God, about life, the nature of mankind and our own hearts as human beings. The Gospel of John is a wonderful place to start. You'll be amazed what you discover about God, and about yourself.

Chapter 15

ometimes it's hard to see where the road of life is leading. But, God often leads us into the unknown. God rarely does things the way we think he should. While we're waiting to do something important, God is doing something important in us. He is refining us. He is making us uncomfortable. Dependent on him. In my mind he is full of surprises. He can't be put into a box, there isn't one that fits him. He is revealing His strength in our weakness. It's a truth that's hard to grasp in the middle of waiting on God to respond. Most of Jesus' life was spent doing what he wasn't sent to do. He was preparing Himself. And if Jesus needed time to prepare, we do, too.

Story after story in the Bible reminds us how God impositions his people, only to position them. He made Joseph uncomfortable in a prison to position him on a throne. He made Daniel lion's food, only to proclaim His glory in the fire. He made Esther prepare her body and heart to be queen, only to position her to save an oppressed people. And He will do the same with you. Because it very well might be that the job you hate or the one you can't find is part of His great plan for your life. He may just use your discomfort to comfort others. God often impositions us in our work, our health, our lives because he is preparing us to position us to reveal His glory.

Sometimes, we think being uncomfortable is a dreadful thing, but after many years of experience, I've come to realize that this was a great part of my growth. A part that I needed more than I would ever know. The word 'uncomfortable' can mean many things. Let me give a few instances. The divorce I didn't want anyone to know about, the federal case that I was put on the news for, the foreclosure, the re-position, turning myself in to a prison to serve my court ordered sentence. Yes, these are just a few of my uncomfortable experiences. I now feel God was making me uncomfortable to prepare me for his version of comfortable.

How many times has He entrusted "Stuff" to me that required me to learn to comfort outside my comfort zone . . . without conditions? How many times has He had to rip things from me because I wasn't ready or willing to surrender them to Him? I thought about all the uncomfortable seasons and scenarios and how He has used *all* of it for my good. Without some of the havoc in my life I wouldn't be willing to be the solider I am in his army. Just to be honest I was a faithful servant in the Devils army and I liked it. Some of the things I've done in my life felt good. I liked it and I won't lie like I didn't. See the thing about many is they play the role that they wouldn't dare do wrong. It's the mask that many share and wear to hide who they really are. But, after some of my life's tragedies I had to sign up for Gods army. I couldn't keep going through this mess with the devil. When I knew for a fact that I could come out with Jesus. The enemy is homeless looking for a place to stay. So, anyone willing to let him live in us without any approval can have at it. But, Jesus has shown me how He has my back and he will never leave me nor forsake me. In my toughest day he will be my strength. But, had I not gone through some seasons of uncomforting I wouldn't have realized any of this.

The truth is, God calls us to live an UNCOMFORTABLE life. Being a believer is not always a glitter and gold. Following Christ is not always easy. Living radically for His name is hardly ever going to be comfortable, and the truth of the matter is . . . it's not supposed to be. Being uncomfortable and suffering for Christ is what we sign up for when we decide to follow Him. Stepping out of our comfort zones and into His will for our lives is what He desires. How would you know you can make it if He never allowed you to have to go through?

 In the times of discomfort, the uncomfortable circumstances He is refining us, making us trust him whole heartedly, perfecting His strength in our weaknesses. Being uncomfortable as a believer means getting a front row seat to see God do some of His best work in our lives and in the lives of others. I want to be right where I can witness that his grace is truly sufficient. Too often we must go on what others say about situations. I want to see Jesus work first hand and what better what than within me.

At times, we take God's grace and his mercy for granted, and now as I look back all the blessings that God had bestowed upon me, that I had claimed the victory for. The blessings I decided to leave him for. He needed to make me uncomfortable, take some things, take me through a storm and allow me to see just discomfort felt. I wonder if I was even ready for all that I experienced, did I even deserve it all? Why did my life have to turn in the blink of an eye? What did I do wrong? How could you do this to me, Lord? And one day I heard it "Why not you?" I needed to be honest, I needed a *real* reality check, because I knew I was heading towards destruction. I had begun to seek money, notoriety, and popularity. I wasn't living for God. I was living for me and living for people to know who I was and what I had. It seems like a warning always comes before destruction, and it always seems to be hard to deal with it. But even in my mess, God was equipping me to make my mess a message. I'm the type that likes to run and hide when the going gets tough. I never knew that I was as strong as I was until I was forced to be. To lose my husband was like experiencing a death, nothing about divorce is easy. Never will be. And just when I thought divorce was the worst part of my story. Then came my federal case. From bad to worst all in a matter of months. You can't ever know just what all another person's endured. That's why now days I'm slow to hear or believe what others say about someone, because more of the time it's a lie. I've seen for myself how people will drag you through the mud just to have something to speak on. Every error a person has made wasn't intentional and most of all isn't always a dreadful thing.

Becoming a teenage mother was one of my best situations. For many it was something to talk about for me it was the start to Gods growth in me. He was born when I was 17, and It was the start to a new kind of love. Soon after his dad became my husband. I wanted to eat what he liked, dress how I felt he wanted me to, fix his food, and make sure he was happy by any means. I had begun to lose myself. I wanted to do what it took to make him happy by any means. And this was the first sign that I was not whole and didn't know what marriage meant nor did I know who I was. Sometimes, your uncomfortable state is needed to teach you about yourself. My divorce taught me so much about me. There were somethings it should me that I wasn't pleased with. I saw some insecure parts of me. Some issues that I needed to heal from and if not, I would be damaging in any other relationship. God made me so uncomfortable see who I was as a wife. It was like I wanted him to blindfold me. Although I wanted to play the role of a wife I wasn't all I could or should have been. I had to learn how to be better for me before I could ever be with anyone else in a union. This was so hard for me to admit, but until I did I'd never be comfortable.

As God is allowing you to learn from your uncomfortable setting, He will always bless you with what you need. At that time, I thought it was money, but it wasn't, because that would have been too easy. He gave me patience, faith and obedience. He carried me through struggles, so I could understand that life wouldn't always be smooth. He sent me faith, so I would trust Him in my darkest hour, He sent betrayal, so I wouldn't trust everyone, He allowed me negative exposure so I would be wiser in my actions. It was almost as if He was saying, "People need to witness your mess so when I bring you back to be a witness for Me they will know that I endorsed you and not man." It was clear to me very quickly that I needed every uncomfortable moment because without it I wouldn't be telling you any of this right now. Help Me! I'm Uncomfortable.

Chapter 16

W̲e all love a great blessing a come up or getting to the next level: We get the check in the mail, the new car, the new job, move into the new house, fall in love blessings are just exciting. We are often excited and contribute it to God. But, from my own experience lately I've been able to add some burdens to my blessings. With every blessing comes a burden. Life seems to be full of contradictions. Honestly speaking I feel we want the blessing without the burden; that's not Gods reality, they come as a package deal. The key is to learn to celebrate the blessing with your burdens. I don't feel we will ever be without burdens and some burdens will never disappear. Lord knows it would be ideal to have the big house without the big mortgage, if nobody ever gossiped about you, no conflicts, no stress, no bills. God wouldn't give you the blessing if you couldn't handle the burden. The real question is, what are we focusing on? We can't focus on the burden and miss our blessing, it would be unfair to God.

Don't pray for a bigger blessing if you're going to complain about a bigger burden. Life is a journey; after you accomplish one goal, there'll be another mountain to climb, another set of burdens to deal with. Don't get lost in where you're going that you miss the greatness of the moment; We must take the good and the bad and enjoy the season were in. Life will never be without something adverse going on. If we watch the news it flooded with mess every day. We don't have to look at the news we can look into our lives, friends live, or families lives and see so much hurt, adversity, brokenness, and pain.

We could be in one of the best seasons of our life and not realize it, because were too focused on what we don't have, how long it's taking, someone else's blessings. Instead of enjoying our blessing, we allow the burdens to weigh us down verses celebrating I all. We try and rush through our season and with that we often miss some of the needed lessons. Here me anything with God has a blessing attached. We can't always see it now, but his intentions are what's best for his children as yours are for your children. It doesn't always feel good to discipline your children, but you have great intentions for them. God wouldn't have you there if wasn't something good on the other end of the season. When you change your perspective, and not focus on the burdens, start focusing on the blessing, then you'll enjoy your life, and not just endure it.

I've come to accept that burdens accompany my blessings. The remarkable thing is that we are all in good company because everyone can relate if they are honest. It's a reality that as I looked back on all the good happenings in my life, I could pair them with some hardship, sad days, struggles, and some tears. If you know a little about the Bible, let's look at the case of the lady with the issue of blood. She bleed for all that time before she got her miracle. Look at Mary and her miracle baby. She was a virgin ready for marriage and she had to accept the fact of being pregnant and judged. Now we all know that she was a virgin, but she had to go through the burden of the haters, judgment and hurt to get the biggest miracle of her life and ours. See, if you look back over your life, you would see that your marriage is a blessing, but the trouble you face is the burden. About having that new baby, the stretch marks, the morning sickness and the contractions are the burden before the miracle arrives.

We don't want to suffer, and we don't want to go through tough times. We only want the blessings and the miracles, not the burdens and the misery. I've lived years, and I just realized that you can't be healed if you've never been sick, you can't be brought up if you've never been down. This chapter is such a reality check for not just you but me. We must understand that God must allow us to see for ourselves, people can tell you anything, but there is something about experiencing life for yourself. The test of your situation does not need any aborting before you get to the promise land. We are always willing to give up and walk away because it's so easy to do that. Suffering has never been easy, but it can be worth it.

I was thinking about how many wealthy people that commit suicide, and realized that it is more proof that blessings can bring burdens. If you search your Bible, you will see that every miracle had some misery. Often, we forget to discuss the burdens and the struggle because we only want to focus on the good, not the bad. Life has a way of showing us that we are not in control and how we deal with it is up to us. The world will continue spinning daily no matter how rough and tough it gets for us. We don't get a stop-life button, and we for sure can't pause life, so this means we must put on the full armor of God, stay prayed up and fight through life with all we have. He never said the weapons wouldn't be formed He said they wouldn't prosper. The enemy is fighting with all he has, and he has no new tactics, he uses what he knows will get to us and he tries it repeatedly when we least expect it. Look back over your life and look at all you've made it through and all you thought would have killed you, and say out loud, "Every miracle required some misery and a blessing required a burden". I honestly want to speak so much further on this, I feel that some situations were unfair, I feel I've been misused and mistreated but regardless of this, I'm blessed. If I was to keep a score of each person I helped back on their feet, I could say

He gave me so much in that season. When people talked, He gave me so much life to stand on my feet, that it really wasn't worth my worry. It all went hand in hand. Although I learned from it, and gained more wisdom, that was priceless. Take it all for what it's worth and know that even those who pretend that there is no misery or burden in their life are not realistic. We all must suffer and go through no matter race, job, education we all have our situations that we must overcome and endure through. Help me! I have been blessed with some burdens attached.

Chapter 17

When I think of the word 'dead', I always think of losing a loved one or someone I know. When we look up the word 'dead', it means *no longer alive*. This definition can apply to so much more than a person. It can apply to situations that we've allowed to live past their expiration date. It can apply to so many of us on the inside. I can for sure apply to many of our dreams and goals. Too often we are the reason that 'stuff' lingers in our lives because we get comfortable and we have become complacent about where we are, and what we've been dealing with, and I can honestly say that it comes with some fear, some low self-esteem, and past issues. The fear of being alone, starting all over, what went on when the last situation ended, how hard it will be to start afresh. All these are common statements that you and I may have used in the past to protect us from dead issues. I've spoken to so many people who are literally dying on the inside all they need is to make the arrangements and to be buried. They have no hope, they are deeply depressed and most have no real relationship with God. They can no longer hear Him and with this are going down a dead-end road. The reason so many of the people I speak to are relatable is because at a point I was a part of the walking dead. No not the show but heck my life just needed a casket and a plot. The thing is I was in good company. But, at some point I had to say I will live and not die. I had too much to press forth for. I had to be healthy mentally and overall.

We have all been in situations where we are in Christ Jesus, but God allows a circumstance or an experience to come about that place us in a valley experience and the experience causes us to evaluate some dead and dry situations in our life. And just like Ezekiel He causes us to roam about them and to visit those situations physically, mentally, and emotionally. (And He caused me to pass about around them and there were many. When in a dead space in your life to take control, you must see what all has you at the point of death. Remember we are speaking about dead situations. You must be willing to sit and be honest to make the decision to live again. But look at what God tells Ezekiel to do when he notices the dry bones. He doesn't tell him to ignore them. He gives instruction that causes Him to activate His faith. He says…. "Son of Man can these bones live?" Ezekiel didn't limit God in His answer…He said Lord, only you know! And God told Him to prophecy to these dry bones and say to them O your dry bones, hear the Word of the Lord!"

What's dry & dead in your life today? Do you feel like your career is dead? Your marriage is dead? Your dreams are dead? Your friendships are dead? Your ministry is dead? Or, are you like Israel during this time and your hope is dead? So, some of us have been so caught up and consumed in a depressed state that we don't even want to get up and live. This is one desperate times call for desperate measure. This is when you must really seek God and cry out for a real deal revamp of life. You can't allow the enemy to win. You have declared greater over your life. See, when you have others depending on you, giving into the plot of the enemy can't stand.

Whether it's the job that you've been on for fifteen years, the person you've been dating for six years, a broken heart, or that friend you grew up with who you can no longer relate to. Whatever must be buried to save you must go. You can no longer allow the devil to suck the life out of you. Dead situations will kill us, and the reality is that the longer you allow it to suck life from you, it will begin to spread like a virus. And slowly cause harm to your life. The fact that dead situations are familiar to all of us, if we're honest enough to admit it. We begin to give up, allowing our thoughts to fill out our death certificate, planning the service but still allowing the body to lie around, wondering what will take place if we buried it. We must decide once we know we've had enough. Call the funeral home back and say I will live. This is not the time for my demise. But, some of this mess that's killing me must go and now.

The most common of these situations that I have heard of are in relationships, there is nothing like a broken heart and damage soul. So many people are together due to comfort, and they don't want the other person to be with anyone else or the fear of being alone and starting all over again. What will people say if we're not together? We tend to use sex to keep us together. Good sex will have you thinking a dead situation has to stay alive. Don't let your emotions keep you in a dead situation. Most of us know when we're dying inside but won't allow the first step of moving on.

We must be wise when we're considering the opinion of others for our lives. The problem is they don't live in your misery, they don't know the death certificate has been signed for the last three years, and you're too concerned about their opinion than your happiness and peace. Most of us won't walk unless it's by force, meaning; the job fires us, a person walks away from us, or God steps in and saves us from ourselves.

Often, we deal with issues in the wrong way, we don't communicate, we're not honest. We are willing to suffer and allow dead and expired situations to get the very best of us. I've realized that burying situations when we know it needs to be done can result in so much heartache and pain at the end. Don't suffer from dead situations and die with them. It's like a parasite and it's taking the life out of us and the sad part is that many know it situations are killing us. We see it, and we allow it. What is within us that is causing us to accept our death? That is what we need to come to grips with, and we must seek God for deliverance. Unless God says allow a dead situation to live let it die.

Take hold of the dead things today. Grab your life back, desire to live and not die. Say aloud and know that your worth way more than the dead things you're holding onto, I'm telling you take your life back and when it no longer hinders, then you know the situation is buried, and you are headed to the repasts of the issue. Help me! I need to bury all the dead situations in my life. Don't die but live a life worth living.

Chapter 18

E xe's are a topic that we should discuss in totality. We must address some issue to realize that some situations are not acceptable or feasible. I've come to realize that exe's can be a blessing and or a curse. Breaking up can be tough. Most people never thought it would hurt as much as it did. They never thought the ending of something that you felt would last was here in reality.

Most of the time we feel that their issues are perfect imperfections and we ignore a ton of the signs that should have been addressed a long time ago. Many of us will stick around past our break up date with hopes it will work or get better and guess what it usually doesn't. We tend to put our issues on the back burner and ignore some issues until we overload. After a certain age we make plans together that makes sense.

Until one day, it hits you: It wasn't just a few small problems. We are different and looking back over it, we were never compatible, we didn't get along and I couldn't do this forever. Suddenly, you realize that you never could have been together in a stable relationship. There were so many signs that showed you the breakup was evident. Suddenly there becomes distance between you. We often become exhausted from dealing with issues and ignoring them over a period. But, what's the point? You're not growing? They're not growing? Why stick in something that you have come to see won't last.

That's because the hardest part about breaking up is convincing yourself that you need to do it in the first place. Sure, we know this decision is for the best, but that doesn't mean it's going to be easy. You feel distraught, because you keep being reminded of it all by a song on the radio, or a bench you ate lunch on together, or a little trinket they gave you that you found behind your bed. And amid all this, *you keep wondering was it the right move*, or did you rush to the demise of your relationship.

It took everything in me to finally realize that *it's totally normal to break up if a person is not the best addition to your life*. Sometimes, the right decision is the most difficult. I couldn't "fix" my feelings. One of the wisest decisions is to never be the first person to date a man after he breaks up with an ex. It's been shown to me that typically the bad karma will be handed to the new boo. It's tough to have a healthy relationship with an angry, jealous or dysfunctional ex. Who wants to deal with all the intentional abuse that they pretend isn't due to the break up?? Therefore, before the start of a new relationship we should all be willing to discuss exes and essential information that may affect a healthy relationship. A ex can make or break a relationship is they are still dying silently and trying to secretly destroy a new relationship. If you can't control an ex or you know they are not trying to let you be great and you're not strong enough to control them. Don't allow them to cause stress to an innocent bystander. Its easy for someone looking in to say don't allow someone else to ruin your relationship. But, honestly there is only so much a person can and should take.

An ex can be a wife, husband, girlfriend, boyfriend, sugar daddy, situatuionship, baby mom or dad or just a thrill. At times everyone's interpretation of the relationship doesn't match, which can cause issues for future relationships. A clean breakup with concise communication can be important, to relay the issues and the cause of breakup can be helpful. No, this can't be done with every relationship due to some ending on a bad note. But, when we can its can be an immense help to eliminate issues.

Never allow an ex to control a new relationship or burden you or your new mate. When a relationship ends the old mate is now null and void. Now, there are some situations where you can't throw the whole ex away but there must be boundaries set. When boundaries aren't set the ex feels they have leverage to control your new situation. This can cause big problems and even breakups. Be willing to be your mates comfort and reassure by showing them that they have you and your undivided attention. Happy is healthy.

There are some situations where an ex is still a part of your life and this is typically coming when children are involved. It usually means there is a co-parent/co-family situation. This is highly recommended for the children and healthy for them. A breakup shouldn't call for adults to be at odds, but many times parents don't have a good relationship after break ups. Typically, when relationships are bad with co-parents one or more parties try and cause issues in new relationships. They often also try and set rules that are tough follow. Typically, this is a sign there are still feelings one or more parties.

Baby moms and baby dads can be a hazard in new relationships. They have a forever relationship that can leave them opportunity to continue to have sexual relationships. And, feel like they have control even after the relationship has ended. This can be a tough situation for the new mate and can cause stress and issues. It can be hard for a parent to balance an ex that is a parent and a new mate that they may have feelings for. It's considering how you're willing to balance all parties, so no one is hurt or mistreated. Cheating can be a damaging thing, so be wise when starting a new relationship and you still have feelings for an ex as well. Often, we try and throw a little side sex in when we have children, and this make a person feel they have control and leaves you in a compromising position.

It's best to be sure that you're ready to date after a break up it can be damaging to deal with a person not sure of how you really feel. It's always best to let all parties know what you want and expect honesty leaves no one to wonder. Consider how you would feel in all dating situations if someone mislead or mistreated you by misleading you in a relationship. Always be aware that you ex should have no control of your new happiness or relationship.

Chapter 19

T his book couldn't have come at a better time in my life. It's truly my life that God has blessed me with. This is the script that God wrote just for me. I'm sure by now you know, I'm pregnant with my first daughter and fourth child. For a few months, I was so embarrassed because I'm ministering and speaking, and people are listening; and now I must reveal I'm pregnant and unmarried. Now let's be clear I never knock people's habits, or try to force people to do anything. Why would if God doesn't. You'll never hear me say don't have sex, don't date, or don't eat meat. That's just not Me. I minister more in a manner that is real to the common person, I've heard people call me a street minister. I'll take that because most people who won't go to church will hear me. I speak truth but don't force my beliefs. I think my transparent method of ministering is how God uses me to touch his people. And I'm loving it. I don't mind sharing my real life, because you can't judge me. Well, you can but it doesn't go very far, just like I can't judge you. It's tough for us to judge one another and we all sin alike. You may not do what I do, or you may and just not be as transparent as God made me. It's alright that's why he made one of me and one of you. But, I must get back to sharing about Princess Kinsley.

I am so embarrassed or just worried about how people will react to me being pregnant and not married. Well, many thought I was dating and knew who I was dating, and I'm sure assumed we were having sex or maybe not. Who knows. Really therefore I speak on not being in people's business. But, you'd be surprised at what people try and figure out in other people's lives. I honestly contemplated aborting my baby. I was fishing for the right plan to make sure this didn't become another ruin me plot for my life. I sat and thought maybe I could keep it a secret and not allow the world to know that I was out here fornicating. And then it hit one day while walking, why does it matter what people think about what you really are doing. It wasn't a concern while doing it so why make it a big deal now?

One day, while I did my morning walk, God said: "When will you stop living for people and live for me. This baby is ours, and she's from me, you may not be married but I'll use this for my glory. See, here I was trying to play God and figure out his plan for my life when he already had it figured out for me. The problem is I didn't know what the plan was. And with me being control the freak I am. That often bothers me about God, why can't he just let me in on what He is doing in my life. Don't have me out here guessing on what he can just tell me. Wouldn't that be great?

So, the more I walked the more we talked this is how our relationship is. We talk like friends. He stated I could have given her to you 16 years ago, even 9 years ago, maybe even 6 years ago, but I saved her for NOW. He later sent two ladies to confirm that some healing will take place with her, some lessons will be learned, some forgiveness will take place, and most of all the anointing would be carried on through her. Not only was I going to birth a baby, but also a new me. I knew somethings were changing in my life during my pregnancy, but I was lost with his plan. I realized that my time with Him was becoming a necessity and not a force. I see myself becoming more secluded and spending more time to know me. I began the book that I was avoiding for so long, and I knew so many people would be healed by reading. This will be the end to a new beginning. A ton of hurt will be endured in this season, but a ton of growth will be birthed as well. My baby is due on 1-01. The word New was once again before me! I didn't have a clue why new was constantly before me. Or what this new thing really meant. But, I was here for it. All of what God was doing for me and my new baby.

The new year will bring new life to my family! I continue to hear the word, and I daily celebrate the new things she will bring. There is so much being birthed right now. I want to know how to love as a mother, I know how to provide for them but I'm unsure of how to be the loving mother I desire to be. I want to see where I need healing and how to be the greater me. I no longer want to be bound by people. And most of all I want to learn how to love. Remember this was one of my lacks growing up. It may sound strange but I'm in good company. Just because we have babies doesn't mean we know how to properly be a parent. So many of us have children but no clue of how to properly love, show compassion, discipline or love. It's because in some instances we lacked it ourselves. How can you give what you properly never had? We know how to give material things and the necessities. But we don't really know how relevant and impactful we are as parents daily, and the duties we are to take on with children.

I'm forever grateful for this experience, for every kick, for every prayer that we are sharing in our prayer closet. We worship together daily. She is a growth spurt for me as a mom and a person. The compassion and love that I'm able to give is being nurtured daily and it's needed not just for her but the boys too. They need compassion, love and need to be taught that they can be sensitive when needed as well. I've been a strict mom because I don't want them to fail or fall short This pregnancy has me in a mushy parenting space. I feel it's because we parent girls different. But, I'm getting the boys need this side of me also. One day they will be future husbands, mentors, leaders and fathers this will set a foundation for them. I never would have thought of the need if I wasn't pregnant with her. She is getting a different side of me. I'm older now and my views are so much different. I've experienced things and want to prevent or at least prepare them for them. I never want them to travel some of the roads I've traveled. Or even endure some of the experiences.

I don't even want them to make some of the choices. I know I won't be able to prevent everything, but I can try.

We must be careful about the foundation that we lay for our kids. It's so important for their future and the people who will be in their lives. Life can leave us bitter and hurt and this can be bad for those who we later deal with and for us. I remember saying to my dad often, "I love you and he never replied, but one day, we talked, and he said he never got that growing up. Something that we assume are standard aren't. Because he lacked hearing I love you growing up, so did I. He knew that he didn't get it in his foundation, so he didn't know how to give it to us. This isn't a fault just a lack of knowledge. Parenting doesn't come with a manual so were trial and erroring through our daily existence. As a young lady, I needed to hear I love you even knowing he did, certain things are essential. I knew without a doubt he loved me more than life he just didn't know.

So, with this pregnancy I began to dissect how I was raised. I started seeing how I was raising the boys. And with this pregnancy I was being revealed to myself as a person and parent. She is helping me with each month. I want to be better for all of them. And daily I can see the change that I want to see. This pregnancy is tough, but I know it has so much purpose and growth attached. Every inch she grows is stretching me as well. Some days I wonder why do I see such a change in me. Why am I so in tune with God and so committed to being better? She is preparing me in ministry there was so much to be said. I am in season of seclusion like I'm in a dessert. Crying our more interceding more for others and most of all my relationship with God is flourishing. I first thought I was hiding the pregnancy, then it hit I was hiding in God. I am hearing clearer and seeking answers on how to be healthier. Not in my physical body alone but my entire life. I starting to love me more and become my whole self. I would not be in the space without this pregnancy. Its birthing me more and more each month.

I pray this book will be a help to someone. I pray that you to sit and realize where you're crying out for help in your life. To know where your foundation has cracked and needs to be repaired. We must be honest, and we must see where we are falling short. It's easy to see the shortcomings of others, but many of us are a disaster to ourselves. Where in your life are you screaming HELP ME?

Chapter 20

M arriage is supposed to be sacred. Marriage is the process in which two people make their relationship public, official, and permanent. It is supposed to be the joining of two people in a bond that putatively lasts until death, but this practice is now more than ever being cut short by divorce. Over the course of a relationship that's supposed to last forever a lot happens. Personalities change, bodies age, and love for one another changes with issues. And no marriage is free of conflict. What allows couples to make it is how they make it through adversity.

I was married for seven years. I never really knew the meaning of marriage, I just knew that I wanted the big wedding and the glam and glitz but was I ready? Marriage is more than just a show. Marriage is the ability to withstand the test of time. But, if you're not in the marriage for all the right reasons then will you be able to withstand? I was excited to have a popular man and I was willing to adjust according to his needs. I was willing to lose me to keep this life alive for other people. We don't always have the right intentions for a forever relationship, but we speak what sounds good for others. And, for many we have the mind to do the right thing in our marriages, but it doesn't always go like this.

You may have heard of that great scripture before. "He who finds a wife finds a good thing." It has two implications: 1. that the man is to do the finding (and consequently, the pursuing); and 2. that the wife is the good thing. I don't want to tie you all up with my analogies of marriage. This section is for the women who may have forgotten how powerful you are. And for the man who desires to be a husband. Or that person who is battling the fact they may never want to marry.

First for the women who may have grown tired of waiting on a man to find a good thing, you're in great company. Many who have been waiting for the perfect man to find them don't get weary in well doing. Well, that's what most people would say. But, when you feel you have it all together and you have yet to be found by your husband this can be tough. And, this is when we begin to play around, get desperate and start doubting yourself. You have it all together you look good, you get likes on social media, men say the right things, you have a career and bloop. You're still single and this isn't what you desired for your life. So, what are you to do? Just hold out baby he's coming. I hope…

What I find most often is that we as women want to be found so bad that we start doing the seeking. We go to the club, events and social media to be found. We attempt to position ourselves in the paths of men we think would be good for us. Professionally astute men with degrees and nice clothes, nice cars and ones who look well put together. We become our very own dating site. We post the good-looking pictures on social sites, the filters that are part "Holy" and a little 'Freaky' we don't want our pastor or church friends to think were soliciting a husband. But, we really are. Heck its been season after season and many have yet to be cuffed. And the spirit of lonely is taking over day after day. See, this is a bad itis to get the lonely itis. It will have you in the bed of the wrong man say he is the one and you know he's not. This is where you must really cover yourself in prayer and seek God. This isn't easy, and I won't act like it is. But, lets help today.

He who finds a wife...

Sis, stop playing hide and seek for your husband. Meaning stop looking for him. No matter how much you try to play like you're not, trying to set it up by likes on post, you trying to trap a man, and you actively seeking a man is you looking for one. See, we try and play mind games for the world so, we will convince our self that we are not looking for a husband when we are. The word states nothing about women seeking out to be found by the man, but the man is to find you. Based on the word a man is led by God to find his good thang, when he prepared. The man is sent out to seek his wife and once found, the man obtains favor from the Lord.

The problem with us women looking for men, is that 1. We're not allowing the man to be the man and fulfill his role; and 2. We're approaching and finding men that haven't yet been completed. He has not found and is not looking for a wife because God is still working on him. You are finding him, won't make him any more prepared and it won't make you his wife.

Instead, much like the man, you should be being prepared in Christ. Us women should be seeking God to prepare us to be ready. Many of us aren't ready to be a wife. Many of us are selfish, have trust issues, insecure and will be a burden as a future wife. We must be prepared as well.

Right now, there are many counterfeits, it's important to dissect what marriage means to you. As you start to feel the desire to be married I need for you to ask God to remake you and help you understand what it means to be a man as a husband and a woman and as a wife. We need to be educated on what its meaning is and what it comes with.

Now, for the man who has the desire to be a husband, but it seems like everyone is taken, into partying ever weekend, twerking, or looking for someone to provide only. You are in good company as well. There are good men left and you may be one. Don't get weary in well doing. You must keep praying that God allows you to find your good thang. And yes, men get lonely too. "It is not good for man to be alone, I will make a helper suitable for him." These were the words of God in the garden before the Lord made Eve. Therefore, it is a good thing - and by the way, a God thing, that a man finds his wife and marries her. When he finds one - he has found a good thing - and has obtained favor from God. What I find interesting though about this proverb is that it does not say, "He who finds a good wife finds a good thing." Many would like for this passage to say this - but it does not. Let's look at this for a few moments to obtain wisdom on the favor

God gives us favor when giving us a wife. The Hebrew word for "finds" in this opening sentence is "masa" which means not just to find, but also to obtain. The word means more than just stumbling upon something. The idea of finding here means that someone is searching for something. In this case what the man is searching for is a wife from the Lord. That is the key here. When he obtains one - it is a very good thing he has gotten. Think about the kind of wife God would have us have - especially if we find one that is according to wisdom. This woman would be of the Proverb 31 kind - she would be a godly woman - and one who delights in her biblical role. Therefore, finding her is a good thing! Since good here means something beneficial - something that makes us happy, glad, and joyful - this is a lady that came to us from God as His provision for a wife. So, this means begin praying for your ability to find your wife. Not just to have sex but to find your own good thing. And that she is sent from God. You deserve your favor.

For that person who is unsure on what you want when it comes to marriage you're also in good company. So, many that have been married and divorced, the individual who may still be hurt from a previous relationship, or that person who only desires to play and never be committed this is not a terrible thing. It's your decision and until it changes its safe not to damage someone's child because you have some relationship issues. What we do is begin to listen to others tell us what we need to be doing, allowing people to set us up and speak what God said to them for us. One thing about it is if God can tell someone else for you He can tell you as well and confirm for you. We need to be mentally ready and healed and released from the past, before we just marry. Make sure your heart is in it. Make sure you're ready and most of all that its your decision to do so. I've always said it easy to get into and hard to get out of. Marriage is a bond that is meant for those who are sure not those who just want a ring or the title. Being that so many live for others seeing your friends get engaged and married doesn't mean its your time its theirs. Use wisdom when committing to God, family and friends in a union that's supposed to be forever not until life get rough, or to someone better comes along. Take your time and be ready in your own way to be a husband or a wife.

Chapter 21

W hy are you here? When I say here I mean why do you exist? Why are you alive? The problem is so many don't have a clue. You're just existing doing what the world tells you daily. Getting up going to work, going to church, eating, in a set routine. Never really stepping out of what you've been told or programed to do. Do you even know what purpose is? Purpose is the reason for which something is done or created or for which something exists. This is profound to think that at some point we should know this answer. To many this may be a hard question to answer. And to some you've discovered it. This isn't a right or wrong answer type question, its one you have yet to discover.

Many of us work so much and are so busy that we've never even stopped to think why we were born. We go through life working 100,000 hours just to die. This can't be Gods purpose for your life. Often, we don't take the time to think about the meaning of our life. But, one day it may hit you because someone is speaking on it or you just want better and then you say there must be a purpose for my life—something we were meant to be here for. Is it to help children, cook, lead, teach just what am I here for? Thoughts like these can come to our minds at transition periods of our life: when we leave home, get a new job, get married, have children, have an empty nest or retire. I'm here to say it doesn't take a life change to know why you're living because tomorrow may be too late. One of the wealthiest places is the cemetery, why you ask, because so many died with great ideas, purpose and gift who never decided to live it out.

What I can assure you of is this. You weren't just born to work, struggle and exist. There is something you were born to do. And the fact that so many, waste time complaining and being afraid to fail or try this my friend is b.s and I'm letting you know to stop wasting life. Get your you together. Sit and decide that you need God and you want to discover why God blessed you to live. Sit and determine why you are here. Expand your horizons and go for it. Look at yourself and decide that no matter what life looks like or what your failures are you go for the best you. Seek your direction for your grand purpose. Don't be afraid to fail it's a part of life this teaches us to try again. I've seen so many people seeking degrees, money and nice cars this isn't all life is about. What are you doing with what you have. We all have our own talents and goals we just must live out the plan. One thing about your purpose is that when it's yours and you're in your own lane this is no stopping you. Too many people who haven't discovered their purpose and decide to jump in another person's lane and can't see why things aren't going right know it's because it's not yours.

Even more, questions about the purpose of life come when we lose a loved one or friend. Being reminded of our own mortality can lead us to analyze our lives and seek deeper meaning to it all. Death can be a total eye opener all the way around. You will decide a whole new plan of action seeing someone close lying dead. But, most of the time this is just an emotion for many and we never reach down to see just why we exist. Life is a gift that we too often neglect and take for granted. Don't allow life to pass you by just sitting and doing what the world feels is best for you. Discover you now. It's never too late to see why you are alive and begin to live it out. Knowing our purpose gives direction to our lives. A life full of purpose is a life of vitality, excitement and ultimately success.

I found my purpose a few years ago at a life class I took with a group of ladies. The teacher the grand Ms. Leland. She began to ask what was our purpose. I didn't have a clue never had even thought about it really. Just going through life doing what I felt was best. But, she guided us all to see what our purpose was, and boy was it life changing. My purpose is to empower and motivate. If you are around me your bound to have a change of heart to be the best, you. I don't care if you've been in trouble, you use to be this, you've done that, you don't have money, no car, no vision. God gave me the purpose to help people see life as a golden egg and I love to do so. I inspire people who have lost hope. I don't have a eye to judge you but I will help you. If that class done nothing else, it taught me that knowing why you exist is so essential to your existence. Otherwise we are out here living for what others are pushing us to live for. When you walk in all you are called to do it's a blessing. God has shown me that the purpose I discovered has helped me to walk in my calling and accept the anointing I have on my life. Help me Lord I need to know my purpose.

Chapter 22

In the previous chapters I wanted to see how I could help my readers in many chapters I spoke truth and tried to help each one of you be better. Now, I'm here. This book has taken a turn. I've explained how life can change from moment to moment and now it has once again. Life has changed for me. There is a lot that God gave me to help others in this book, but from this point on, I feel that God wants to use this book to Help *me*. There is purpose in this pain. As you will see, my words will be transparent so that they can be blessings the readers. There was a reason for the months of writing through my pregnancy, I could have never known Gods plan was this. *If there is anything I could give to help my readers here it is.*

So, here we *grow*. On November 1st the pregnancy I spoke of in the previous chapters became my *Help Me* moment. Kinsley Airelle! Yes, that is the special angel's name that God handpicked for his garden. Sympathy isn't what I desire, growth and wisdom is what I feel God is giving through me. Nothing was easy about the moment I heard my OB/GYN tell me that the child I had carried for eight months didn't have a heartbeat. Or the look on his face as he stood before myself and my loved ones to disclose that we had a fetal death. Now, I heard the words roll off his tongue. My instant reaction was I had been faithful to God and he does this to me. My instant thought was I've prayed for your people, I've spent more time with you, I changed some of my ways and this is what you do to me to us. Why would you allow me to go eight months God, why not let me miscarry at 6 weeks, 9 weeks. You knew I contemplated abortion why did you tell me you gave her to me. Why this? It seemed that God was silent. My doctor told me that I had to deliver. I had to push this baby out. I recalled I had done a live called push in the pass, it was about not being able to quit but pushing through. I was here in a push moment. I won't lie I was angry honestly, I still am. I asked God before the funeral why did you take my baby? It's so many other pregnant women and you take our baby. He then Spoke She is my baby I loaned her to you. I got quiet. He reminded me how I had ministered to people who had suffered losses of all kinds during my pregnancy and encouraged them and spoke of Job. He put Job before me and with all of me I could curse a God who had never left me nor forsaken me. So, here I stood trying to hear God clearly and trust him in my darkest hour.

Reality was sinking in I would never get to rock this special little girl to sleep, take her to the park, dress her for church, take her to school, or ever say prayers with her. The pain I felt at 9:30 a.m. on November 1st, 2017 must have added purpose to the pain I already bore. I had so many questions for God. I needed to know what I had done wrong? Did I miss hearing Him? Why did He give me just what I asked for, and then just snatch it from me? How do I handle a pain of this magnitude? I felt I had done it all right. I was trying to eat better, I was even walking daily, I prayed and worshiped with her faithfully and I was so happy. But most of all, I was at my faithful point with God. And for me to be standing there wondering where my faith stands regarding a God that had brought me so far, was tough to say the least. I was angry, sad, numb, and lost and wanted to blame the world. This couldn't be what God had planned for me. But, in retrospect it was. He allowed me 3 days with her. She laid on me, I gave her bath, I prayed with her, and loved on her. I witnessed God pouring strength into that I never had. A familiar verse was quoted to me it so familiar but the light in which it was shed gave me a different trust in God. Romans 8:28New King James Version (NKJV)

^{28} And we know that all things work together for good to those who love God, to those who are the called according to *His* purpose.

Let's look the word "All" things work together for the good of us, me, you who love God. Which meant that All means everything, nothing left off. Not this death of Kinsley, not the pain I feel, not the anger in me. It all works together for the good of those who love him. I know for a fact that I love Him. And I know that his words are stating above that although it looks bad and may even feel bad that it will be good for me in due time because I love him.

If trusting God regardless of the situation was what I'd have to do, then He was for sure going to have to show me how. I know that He was only lending her to us, but why was He taking her so soon? Was I to be selfish and ask if there was someone else He could have chosen? He handpicked her and this was nothing we could control or change. We've all heard the story of Job, but if not, it's a story about a man who lost everything he loved and cared for and still he wouldn't dare allow himself to curse God. His faith in God after being tested by the enemy was still unshakeable.

Job knew too much about God to doubt Him. Even after losing his children and all that he had, he desired to trust God with all of him. No matter what his friends and wife said he still wouldn't curse God. Was this my Job test? Could I do this? Was I even strong enough? Did God trust me this much? It was clear to me that God has a wager on me. The enemy was trying to convince me to come back to his team, he wanted to doubt God plans. He said How could God take your baby. I thought He knew it all. Could he not have saved her, by removing that cord. In my heart I feel that God will never take anything and not give you more in return.

For me I had to pray, I had to hear God. I needed to understand the pain I was enduring, and I needed God to know that I only wanted what He wanted for me. Or was that just what I knew people in our perfect world would need me to say? One wonderful thing about God is that He is all knowing, He is omniscient, He knows past, present, and future. He has a perfect plan for my life, for my children and for Kinsley. Nothing can replace this beautiful angel and I know that only time can heal this pain. The tough part is that with me stating he is all knowing. He knew that he would take her from me at my eighth month. He knew that he would be working on the new me in this time. He was working on so much in me through her and my pregnancy and I wouldn't have done it without his help. Some people may think I'm foolish to be saying this. But, I believe with all of me that there was a reason his plan was like this.

As I contemplate daily, I see that my time is being dedicated more to God. A heart with no beat is so hard to imagine. I realize that in my pain there lies a blessing. I know that there must be purpose in this life lesson even if it's not for me, even if years from now; my experience finds expression in showing someone else how to grieve, how to pray through, or how to trust God by hearing my story. There comes a point where we must break free from the things that hinder us and hold us back. I realize that our weakest moments make us who we are, they make us stronger. I know that God would never intentionally hurt me, He's not that type of God. He's not a God that would ever harm me or cause me to be intentionally hurt. I know for a fact that the love He has for me is so great that He sure has something greater for me. I know that Satan wants to play on our minds and on our hearts. I know that he wants us to doubt God. No matter how much God has brought us through, Satan needs us to doubt what we've seen for ourselves in God. He is homeless, so he needs a place to house pain—the lies, defeat, stress, struggles, fear, worthlessness, suicide, and the plans that he has created. He uses us and what he knows would hurt us. He usually doesn't use anything we won't fall for. He knows the things that will try and hinder us. My children are everything to me, so he needed to try and use the death of my baby to make me question God. He will not defeat me is what I had to say. Our mind is a dangerous place and it's a weak place for so many. You must remember that if you change your thinking you will change your entire life. No pain is pointless and but this is a pain that left me speechless, even thinking about the experience is painful.

For a mother, the excitement of hearing the words "You're pregnant" is life changing. The months pass, and the growth, the bond, and the experience is one you cherish. Never would you consider in a million years that you would not deliver a healthy baby. The mind-blowing thing is that it never crossed my mind. Or did it? For months, as I prayed and worshiped, I heard consistently and very vividly the words: *death*, *die* and *dead*. Was the Holy Spirit preparing me for what was to come? I asked in my quiet time why I was hearing this so vividly and so often, but I just shrugged it off as preparation for the future passing of a loved one. Does God prepare us for what He has planned for our future? Did He need to allow me time to handle this pain? I began to see that God is a jealous God. Was I too consumed by my first daughter? Had I placed her before God? Was God trying to show me something deeper? Did He need to get me in a space that allowed me to need Him and really bond in my time of grief? I love my children - all three boys, and will forever love Kinsley. Nonetheless, I can't allow myself to forget where my greater love lies and that's in the Lord. I've heard that I am a strong woman from so many and I've heard that I will make it. It's not because of my own strength, it's all from the Lord. Nothing in life says "Listen" like God needing you to hear His voice and getting your attention. So, often we miss the message because we try to decipher the message we desire to hear.

This book was to help me birth a dead baby. I had to complete the process. I couldn't abort. Let's leave Kinsley for a second and hear this was He birthing more dead things in my life. I feel that with this so much in me will come forth through ministry. See, with pain you become stronger and wiser. I was speaking to my cousin and he said right now there are so many dead ministries around the world, what you do is speak life to those who feel the church is dead. I know that God has a plan for the pain and I know without it I may have aborted his plan. Now I needed to understand that It's Okay to Grieve!

The way grief affects us depends on you as a person, including what kind of loss you've suffered, your relationship with the person or thing, your beliefs, and your physical and mental state of mind. I don't think it's ever been a time for me to grieve, I never really loss anyone who has caused me to feel the way I currently feel. I must come to realize that it doesn't just mean a person passing is the only loss we suffer from. We need to learn to go through the processes of life in our own way. No one can teach me how to grieve through this process. There have been books given, and I've googled many feelings but I'm truly having to go through this process in my personal manner. Losing a child, I feel may cause you to grieve in a unique way, then a parent or a family member. Although many may feel I never knew her how could this be such a big issue? I bonded for eight months and got to know her as any mother would. I was expecting her and had begun to change my life to include her with my plans and desires. My everyday function was a shared space with her and I loved every second of it. So, to abruptly lose this and my body still have the functions of a mother with a baby it has been tough. I've blamed, felt suicidal been angry and I have battled with God. But, I've also been in a place alone that I rest and feel that I'm getting even closer to God. I go back to every burden comes with a blessing. Well, this burden hasn't been all bad. I decided to grieve and not rush into a healing place. I'm resting and for a change nothing to rush my life but taking it day by day.

We must realize that some people take a lot longer than others to recover from a loss. Some need help from a professional. I always say that your pastor can't always help you get the help you need. Although they are a great outlet professional counselor are really the best way to get the answers needed and professional answers. But you will eventually come to terms with your loss, and the intense feelings will subside. But there isn't a defined time or limit. There's no instant fix.

You might feel affected every day for about a year to years after a major loss. But after this time the grief is less likely to be at the forefront of your mind.

There are practical things you can do to get through a time of bereavement or loss:

- **Express yourself.** Talking is often an effective way to soothe painful emotions. Talking to friends, family members, or a counsellor as needed.

- **Allow yourself to feel your emotions as they come.** It's a healthy part of the grieving process.

- **Finding what allows you peace and a sound mind daily.** Journaling, and reading books.

- **Sleep and Rest as you often as you feel you need it.** Emotional strain can make you very tired.

- **Eat. Often when grieving we don't eat as we should or would prior due to lack of appetite.** Eating will help you cope and have energy.

- **Avoid things that "numb" the pain, such as alcohol.** It will make you feel worse once the numbness wears off.

- **Go to counselling if it feels right for you** – but perhaps not straight away. Counselling may be more useful after a couple of weeks or months. Only you will know when you're ready.

- **Allow your natural sadness not to be suppressed.** Allow yourself to be honest with your body that you are in a state of sadness to heal naturally.

- **Pay attention to your child/children in their grief stage.** Allow them to share their feelings, whether it's through talking, drawing, crying, or games. Children need to feel they are listened to, so include them in decisions and events if it feels right

Only you know how you need to heal. Allow yourself to grieve and go through as need be. Take the time that you need. Spend to time to explore your thoughts and feeling in alone times. Often, we will hide our true feelings when others are around. Really dissect the loss to see what the good things that may have come of this loss. Pray often as you need to. Be honest with God about your feelings to God and how you really feel about him allowing the loss. Just do it is what I recommend more than anything Just Grieve as you see fit. Never rush the process of healing.

I've spoken on a MeTox throughout this book and maybe some got it and some didn't. But here is what you should know about a Metox and it's a needed cleanse for your entire life. For everything you think, for every move you make this is a necessary task.

Some may ask What is a Metox and some may put two and two together and discover it's a Detox for your personal self.

The true definition of DeTox:

Noun:

1.

A process or period in which one abstains from or rids the body of toxic or unhealthy substances; detoxification.

Don't be surprised, but toxins aren't just found in air pollution or eating bad and alcohol consumption. When most people feel they want to feel healthy they plan a detox. But, there comes a time when we all need to do the same for our self. When you feel you need a true release, clarity and glow-up, you must look at all parts of your life. You must evaluate what is toxic specifically to you and cleanse out what is weighing your life down. You must not only look at what you are eating, but what (or who) is eating you.

We should do complete evaluations of our entire life from family, attachments, friends, finances, health, career, dreams. relationships and visions. We are a complete person when we look at everything it reveals us to us. It's like looking at a recipe and deciding to leave some of the ingredients out of it. We can't be the best person we can with toxins. Toxins can be stress, people, dysfunction, drama, anger, and financial issues. But, how do we start the Metox? Start purging. Simplify your life. Get rid of stuff.

Start purging your life. Simplify your life. Get rid of stuff.

May seem hard to do but know that I'm dead serious about this. If you're desiring a change in your life, purging is probably one of the most transformational actions you can make. You just might learn more about yourself than any other self-help activity you've tried.

You've probably purged several times already in your life not realizing it. Life changes require purges. Think about it. If you have ever moved, had a baby, changed careers, ended a relationship or been ill, at some point you must remove possessions, relationships, obligations and spending habits from your life to make that change possible (whether you wanted to or not).

Too often we believe the only method of changing our lives is by adding something new to it. That is true, but at the same time you need to also subtract to create space for that addition. We forget that very important step, so we end up feeling stuck in our over-cluttered lives. This Metox is so important and without it at times it can detrimental.

Let me be clear, I'm not suggesting we get rid of everything in your life, so you can start over (that might work for a few, but it's not for most of you). I truly believe metox is a powerful exercise to bring clarity and focus to your life. It has the potential to show you how much you can learn about your fears, desires, dreams, values, hiccups, passions and motivations.

Anyone who knows me personally, knows how passionate I am about the topic of purging. There's so much I can share with you. My goal here is to introduce the concept and maybe even get you started on your own purge. Don't continue to live a life of destruction it's okay to go through and heal. Some people can do this alone and there are some who need professional help in their healing and never allow anyone to say you're crazy because you seek professional help. It can be the life saver that will change your thinking to change your life. You deserve to live free and whole. There is also purpose in your pain. God is a healer and he desires us to live our best life. This batter where fighting isn't ours and at times we try to do alone. Help Me I want to be whole.

DEVOTION 1

Stillborn Devotions

We all know I'm big on knowing the true definition of a word. Honestly never had a need to know the definition of Stillborn. But, for some reason it's now a desire to know more. It must be something that God seeks for me to know that's deeper than I can imagine. So here it is

adjective

adjective: **still-born**

1. (of an infant) born dead.

    o (of a proposal or plan) having failed to develop or succeed; unrealized.

In my days of being home I've desired to spend as much time with God as possible in a more desperate way. This for me has different because the desire when your desperate for something is like a live or die battle. I started desiring more of the uncut version of God. I feel I can skip the appetizer and head straight to the desert. And today it's like he confirmed something through Kinsley! Not just for me it may help you also. The Holy Spirit revealed to me the word stillborn for several days now. And it hit me that most of our lives are like Kinsley's. We get right to the end, I mean to the finish line and boom a cord wraps around our plans, goals, dreams, and it's over.

The enemy desires to hinder, but we know that. But, what if we cut the cord. What if we allow the Dr. (God) To catch our babies and cut the cord that seemed dead then what? The book, business, vision, dream, goal would live. Something's have hit us, and its goal was to choke our progress, we must grow through it. Today we need to decide 2018 we won't allow anything to choke our vision. We're going to cut some cords and declare life. Although it's not meant for everything to live it's not meant for everything to die. Don't allow fear, doubt, worry and life to wrap around you. There is so much greatness within you. Cord death doesn't have to be the cause of death on your progress. Think past your little dreams and have some big God dreams. And watch God work. No matter what complete the tasks and plans in your 2018 even if it's just you and God. Step out of our comfort zone.

I've seen so many people give up on what they really desired in life due to a setback or a road block. I know from experience that some of my worst situation birthed my greatest victories. But, it wasn't until after the failure and the story ended that I got the true blessing in the situation. All ways remember that every blessing comes with a burden of some sort. Be wise in what you allow the enemy to utilize to abort your "baby". In this season of your life feel free to speak over your "Baby", whatever it is. Even if it means the cord is there and you must make the decision that this "Baby" must come forth. Cut the Cord and keep pushing it will be worth it in the end.

In many of our lives we have some people who are hindering our babies being born. They are still stuck, still hating, still dysfunctional, and holding you back in your life. We must see when people are keeping us from having a healthy delivery. We also must be aware of when that someone is us. We can be a murderer of our best self at times. Be honest and open to see your life in a way that demands healing for a healthy delivery is so important. Decide to live today and know the weapons may form but they won't prosper.

Isaiah 54:17King James Version (KJV)

[17] No weapon that is formed against thee shall prosper; and every tongue that shall rise against thee in judgment thou shalt condemn. This is the heritage of the servants of the Lord, and their righteousness is of me, saith the Lord.

King James Version (KJV)

DEVOTION 2

Life-ache Devotions

To often we have headaches, and some have them more than others. There are even some people who have them to the level of a migraine. This I hear is no fun to have. But the definition per Google is:

Noun plural noun: **headaches**

1. a continuous pain in the head.

synonyms: pain in the head, migraine; More

  o *informal*

a thing or person that causes worry or trouble; a problem.

Now that you know what a headache is let me tell you what a "Lifeaches" is. Sometimes life will bring some for sure low blows and they are accompanied by a pain in the heart that won't go away. The thing about lifeaches are some are inevitable and there are some that we tend to invite, allow and stay past their expiration date. Seeing that I have a continuous pain after the death of my daughter I see that there are some we don't select, but as I look back over my life t

here are some I said, "Hey come on in and stay a while". Its can be a bit mind blowing to know that we self-inflict so much as if we don't care for our wellbeing.

One thing about life is it will not stop it doesn't have a pause button so no matter what this implies we must keep going as well. Life is for sure going to do what it's going to do without our permission. Knowing this says to me that we are forced to boss up and go with life as it comes. There will be some issues that seem to linger longer than others and some that we will shake off in a matter of days. It's our decision how long we stay somewhere that's unhealthy in our lives, mental state in our thinking and growth.

Don't stunt your growth trying to fix life when its not meant for us to figure it out. Too often we will try and fix what got has included in our life package. As you look over your entire life today see where it is that you have some life aches. See, how they got there were they invited by you or inevitable situations. In every lesson we can learn and grow. Sometimes we must just have to tell God he is God and he is the only one who can fix the messes that we allow. He has a solid plan that is guaranteed to be the best thing for us. We just must often trust what we can't see, feel or have any evidence of just to make over some lifeaches.

The migraine level lifeaches are meant to take us out. This is where you see people commit suicide and drive themselves crazy. We can't give the enemy a crack in our door of life or he will slide in and consume your mind and thoughts. Don't allow the enemy to lifehack your situation and convince you your life can't be normal and healthy. You have more control than you would even begin to see. Speak life and encourage yourself in your migraines of life. Tell yourself you are more than a conquer and the enemy has no place and begin to believe what you're speaking and take a pill of God which is 100 mlg of prayer and 100 mlg of the word and healing will begin to take place. Praise will always confuse the enemy Sometimes you're in need of a rescue pill from God, and He desires to be our help. Just like when you have a headache and you go to the pharmacy for meds He's waiting on you to call out for your aspirin of healing and release. Are you willing??

1 John 4:4New International Version (NIV)

4 You, dear children, are from God and have overcome them, because the one who is in you is greater than the one who is in the world.

New International Version (NIV)

DEVOTION 3

Drowning Devotions

I'm not a swimmer, and to be honest I can't swim at all. I'm afraid of the water in my face and ears its irks me to even think of it. We've heard of people drowning and even witnessed it on movies at times. Every time, I've seen it on a movie it seems like a tough death. To see someone battle water in my mind is never winning battle because of the force water has. Let's see what google states about the word:

Drown

verb

gerund or present participle: **drowning**

    1.   die through submersion in and inhalation of water

When I look at this word and its meaning it automatically states the word die, and for many of us we don't realize how we are drowning in our problems and issues daily. Which to me indicates the problems that we are submerging ourselves in can be killing us. We can't stress ourselves with issues that we can't fix no matter how we try in the flesh.

We have all been drowning victims some by choice and some by force, we've been in the pool with no life guard around and no life jacket in sight. It seems that we have no hope of living through this situation and typically this is a crossroad for us. What crossroad you may ask the one where we really trust God or give up on being a believer. And, to be honest it's when the enemy begins to go in overdrive in adding all the issues that have us in the pool of life. He is aware of what we battle with and what will take us to the drowning stage and he isn't here to see us survive. He wants us to crack and doubt the Lord. But, you must be strong in knowing the He is a lifeguard that will rescue us.

He is one that will set the captives free, he heals the sick, he made a way and we often forget and desire to drown verse get to safety. This is where your faith must come in to play. I know it can sound easier than done. But, seeking the word is what we must do when the submerging seems stronger than your will to make it through. At times God will allow us to stay in the pool to strength our faith and trust in him. And, when everyone feels the need to say you're dead he comes through like an expert life guard and pulls you out of the pool of life and lets everyone witness it. At times he needs to see will we believe.

When the you begin to drown, and things begin to be so overwhelming that you don't know if you want to make it, stop and know you're standing in the need of all God can give you. It's not always easy ask for the meds he has. Some feel like it's a specific way He's looking for you to come. He knows how many hairs are on your head, just go like you are. Broken, busted and lost. He's waiting but are you willing.

Hebrews 11:29-31New International Version (NIV)

[29] By faith the people passed through the Red Sea as on dry land; but when the Egyptians tried to do so, they were drowned.

[30] By faith the walls of Jericho fell, after the army had marched around them for seven days.

[31] By faith the prostitute Rahab, because she welcomed the spies, was not killed with those who were disobedient.[a]

DEVOTION 4

Omniscient Devotions

adjective

adjective: **omniscient**

1. knowing everything.

We serve a God that really knows everything. Wait, look at this again. He knows it all. He knew you wouldn't be able to pay that bill. He knew you'd get fired, He knew I'd lose the baby at eight months. He knew the business would close. He knew your spouse would cheat. He knew the house would foreclose. He knew the car would get repossessed. But, why is He allowing all this if he knows all? his I feel is how God builds a relationship with us. He isn't learning anything, He hasn't forgotten anything. Which indicates he does allow dreadful things in our mind to take place. He has His reasons and we may never understand them or feel they are fair.

This I feel is where the learning experience takes place. I feel he allow us to grow through the struggles that he allows. If everything was peaches and cream daily how would you really be? Had you not lost some things, would you really know how to appreciate. Had that marriage not ended would you know what you really needed in your new mate? We must at times go through to grow through. We never are aware of Gods true plans or desires for us, it can be tough to trust when we are going through. Growing pains are never easy, nor are they desired but, we can't say they aren't necessary.

Look at it like this. If God let us know his plan for our lives daily, we would often try and assist him. We would be his way if he revealed all He knows to us. It would be a constant battle with Him trying to teach us and us trying to show him. There is something positive in every set back God allows in our lives.

O LORD, you have searched me and known me. You know when I sit down and when I rise; you discern my thoughts from far away. You search out my path and my lying down, and are acquainted with all my ways. Even before a word is on my tongue, O LORD, you know it completely. You hem me in, behind and before, and lay your hand upon me. Such knowledge is too wonderful for me; it is so high that I cannot attain it (Psalm 139:1-6).

What do you do when you can't trace God but are required to trust him? It would be so great to know what God has going on for us—when we'd get married or remarried, have a baby, get the job, start the business. Just when?

If God gave us our schedule of life and we knew when it would all pop off, not just for us, but for anything involving us, if an alert would go off on your I-phone or Android to notify you, and your life wasn't a mystery. I know however, that what Mel just desired sounds great but it's not a reality.

Then where would faith come in? How would your faith and relationship with God mature? How would you learn to trust a God that you can't feel? Well, here's a good word.

"…because God has said, 'Never will I leave you; never will I forsake you.'" **Hebrews 13:15** NIV

There are times in our lives when we simply can't feel God. No matter how much we invest in prayer, worship, Bible study, etc. We often cry out to God, begging and pleading for His response to no avail, when we feel we need Him the most. But, look at this - I haven't seen in the Bible where it says that He will always be on time (your time). I've never seen where He states that He will always make a way (your way). The easiest conclusion to jump to at, when we simply can't feel God is that He has left us. Remembering that God has already promised to stick with us for the long haul is like the air we breathe to be able to remain faithful to Him, even when we cannot feel His presence.

I realize that this is why so many of us give up, we give up in the waiting stages. In the stages where we must wait to see the manifestation of our prayers, because we are inpatient and listening to gospel greats like *'He's an on-time God yes He is'*. What if you're *on time* isn't God's? Do you then become doubtful? What if His time isn't anywhere close to yours. As a matter of fact, some of us in many situations have yet to witness His *show up*. And so what?

But how do you trust God when you can't hear, see or feel Him? During the time when I couldn't hear God, couldn't map Him, and couldn't see what to do next, I had to learn a few *thangs and quick* that have helped me. When you can't trace God, you can still trust Him. Sometimes He wants to see what you are saying and if we are faithful.

The scriptures are filled with the promises of God. In those times when you don't hear God and you cannot get any direction from Him, turn to His word. His word tells us that He will never leave us or forsake us **(Deuteronomy 31:8)**. So, in the times when He seems far away, you can be rest assured that He is still there.

Remember ALL He did for you.

The reason I'm able to trust God is because prior to the many contracts, I've been penniless and jobless. I've been at low points! But God provided for me - I never went without food, I didn't get evicted, I never had utilities turned off, my car wasn't repossessed.

Worship... Real personal worship

The Bible tells us in **John 4** that our Father is seeking worship. He is actively looking for those who will worship Him no matter what. Instead of complaining and crying and fussing about your situation, worship God. He will show up right where you need Him. In **2 Chronicles 1,**

Solomon needed something from God. He was set to rule a kingdom of people and Solomon had no clue what to do. He needed wisdom. So, Solomon called the leaders together and they worshiped the Lord. AND BAM.. Solomon's worship was so attractive to God that Solomon didn't even have to ask God, God asked Him.

Ask and seek His face

Too often we pray and ask God for things, but when we don't hear from Him, we stop praying. We give up and give in. But Jesus said in **Matthew 7** to ask, seek, and knock. This is a persistent type of prayer. If you can't trace God, sometimes it's because He wants you to be more active in seeking Him. He wants you to be tenacious with your prayers. Don't allow God's silence to keep you from going hard after Him. He's coming, and on His own time.

DEVOTION 5

The battle....

I woke up this morning wondering how in the world I struggle so much with my mind. Now, let me be more specific, how is it that I serve a God that says and has so much for me and I still *half see* it and often *half believe* it. I began to contemplate yesterday on how many conversations I had or messages I received asking for prayers and how many battles my closest friends were in. I began to ask; "Are these self-inflicted issues?" "Have they gone to God in prayer for what their battling?" "Do they believe what God has said about their situations?" "Or do they even believe what He said He will do for them." The conversations were different but similar. Doubt was taking so many to a sunken place. It was obvious that the enemy was winning a battle that we often don't even fight to win. We listen to his lies and play his games and wonder why our kids are being attacked, our marriages are battling, why we doubt our business success, and how we allow mediocre nonsense to take over our days. Lack of consistent prayer and lack of the word is the issue.

After typing for a minute, the Holy Spirit said: "Do you really trust God? You don't have to be a Bible scholar to look back over your life and see when and how God has brought you out. You don't have to be a preacher to seek the word for your own battles." To many of us are self-ordained Doctors prescribing remedies that are only temporary and often; have to be administered over and over, because we're only covering the wound not healing it. As I prayed last night I heard: "The cycles of repetitiveness". I was confused until later. This cycle makes us repeat - offenders of hurt, drama, doublemindedness, mental issues, generational curses, lies, fornication, poverty, broken homes, financial lack, jealousy, insecurity and so much more. We always see it for others, but we suffer these issues over and over personally. At what point do we decide to become consistent in our entire lives? We start and stop everything. We're so inconsistent in our lives. We pray for a few days and read the word, but when life's OK we drop back to what caused us our issues. We may focus on a healthy life for a week but go back to unhealthy lifestyles after days. Healthy lifestyles aren't just working out, together with eating right. It's rest, it's mental balance, it's knowing when your entire life needs a revival.

One thing the devil does is bombard our mind with a cleverly devised plan of little nagging thoughts, drama, suspicions, doubts, fears, wonder, reasons and theories. He moves slowly and cautiously (after all, well-laid plans take time). Remember, he has a strategy for his warfare in your life. He has studied us for a long time. He knows what we like and what we don't like. He knows our insecurities, our weaknesses and our fears. He knows what bothers us most. He is willing to invest any amount of time it takes to defeat us. One of the devil's strong points is patience.

The devil is a liar. Jesus called him *the father of lies and of all that is false* **(John 8:44)**. He lies to you and me. He tells us things about ourselves, about other people and about circumstances that are just not true. He does not, however, tell us the entire lie all at one time. Be wise today with all your situations and thoughts.

Take your life back today. Whatever you're battling, you're in control every second of the day. Don't allow the same tactics and ploys to run your life into a cycle of repetitiveness. Decide today to win. Victory over all your issues are won in Jesus name.

Some of the best lessons in life are the ones you cried over, struggled with, that brought you to your prayer closet, and really forced you to depend on God. Can you think back on the situation that you know only

God could have brought you out of? The one that brought you off prayer vacation into prayer overtime? The situation when at the last hour God showed up for you? Those were the lessons that were blessings. Bad or stressful situations oftentimes force us to seek God, when we had been seeking self for all the answers.

Your *go through* becomes your *grow through* and when this takes place, God knows you need Him most. Nowadays it's easier to seek answers from friends, family or a counselor, when your situation is ordained and purposed and ready for victory. Victory isn't always what we desired as an outcome, sometimes God must be your eyes and ears and be your 'No' when you feel it's a 'Yes'. Sometimes, God must close that door before you walk through it, because you can't see the road ahead. It's not always what we want, but He always has our best interest at heart.

It seems like we can be like gravity, attracted to what we need to run from. We try and force friendship, relationships, jobs, and even financial decisions. When we want something to work we are willing to force it. We don't always look down the road ahead we only see the now. We don't look at the whole picture we look at the part that fits our desire.

Imagine if God hadn't blocked some of the mess He has now shown you He handled for you. There's nothing like Gods protection. Be wise and seek Him in prayer for all your answers, big or small. This is a method for often preventing time wastage, bad relationships, confusion and hurt. Our judgment can often be off when we want something. We're kind of selfish when it comes to what we desire.

Wouldn't it be awesome to wake up every morning and know you're on the right direction in life with zero bumps? To know with certainty that you're headed on the right road? To feel confident with each step, without constantly questioning yourself or situations or people? This would be a *win win* for us all. But, *scuurrrr...* Life isn't quite like that.

Too many times I've second-guessed a decision I was confident about. I want so desperately to follow God's will, that I'll pray but then feel uncertain—not wanting to make a wrong move. I wonder: "Maybe this isn't what I'm supposed to be doing. Maybe this isn't part of God's plan for my life." I doubt when often I should trust. I've messed up too many times seeking my will.

Remember this today, God is the one who understands our past and future—He has knowledge of our weaknesses and strengths. The Lord will protect us, yet challenge us to grow in our Christian walks. So, you must go through to grow.

God will lead us along a path that will fulfil His plans for our lives. But, we must trust Him and seek Him. He is the one who knows the direction we must follow and will lead us accordingly.

God is the source of wisdom for all things. Realize that He not only has the answer, He is the answer. **Proverbs 2:6 and 9** states, "For the LORD gives wisdom, and from His mouth come knowledge and understanding... Then you will understand what is right and just and fair—every good path."

Are you seeking Him?

DEVOTION 6

Some of our lives are just out of control.

Wondering, hurting, depressed, confused, insecure, jealous, soul tied, suicidal, busted, and disgusted. All by choice. At some point you must decide what you like about *what has you stuck*. Some evidence shows that we enjoy our dysfunction. What we speak, who we are around, what we believe, how we act and what we accept can really become a dilemma for us daily. At what point do we get tired of being depressed, lost, and mentally incarcerated? At what point do we begin to not make excuses but create avenues to healthy living. No matter what others are saying to motivate and push you, what are you doing for your true release. Too often we want to be pacified for mediocre nonsense and STUFF that we could have prevented or totally avoided. But, we must decide what we really want and need, to be the best us.

Relationships, friendships, hangouts, habits have us in bad positions, have us unequally yoked, struggling, confused, and addicted to *the unhealthy*. How can we become free from self? How do we change our *stinking* thinking? How do we press for better, no matter what it looks like?

The Bible makes it clear that there are demons, or evil spirits in the world that interfere in people's lives (Ephesians 6:11-19). Evil forces, or powers, influence and control the minds of individuals, bring sickness and cause undesirable behavior, inability to function normally, and even suicide. Because of these forces, people can become a danger to themselves as well as to others who care. I'm not saying that it must be physical, but unhealthy spirits can be transferred if we're not careful. If you look at social media, so many pretenders, fakers and straight up dysfunctional characters prey on you daily, through their influence over what you read and what comes from them that you indulge in.

We must be careful about what we allow daily into our minds, spirits and lives. We must be careful to take heed to the warnings that the Holy Spirit gives us. Be able to discern when to move, speak, listen, and run. We don't even realize that some of this mess has attached to us.

Visualize what I'm about to say. To keep our computers safe from attacks, we try to strengthen its defenses. What can be done to fight off computer viruses? Install a firewall. A firewall prevents our computers from outside threats. It allows the data we consider safe to enter, and blocks the data we don't consider safe from harming our computer.

It's no different with our mind. We must strengthen our defenses by installing a firewall to guard our thoughts every single day.

Proverbs 4:23-27 tells us: "Be careful what you think, because your thoughts run your life. Don't use your mouth to tell lies; don't ever say things that are not true. Keep your eyes focused on what is right, and look straight ahead to what is good. Be careful what you do, and always do what is right. Don't turn off the road of goodness; keep away from evil paths." We must constantly be on the defensive to ward off wrong thoughts.

Isn't it true that our thoughts dictate the direction of our daily lives? The greatest battlefield of life is the mind, and we are constantly at war for its control! If we want to live right, we must put up spiritual firewalls and not allow just anything to affect our thinking. Computer programmers have a name for this process. It's called GIGO. GIGO is an acronym that stands for "garbage in, garbage out" —which means that what you put in is what comes out. What you allow is what you like.

In **Mark 7:20-23,** He said, "The things that come out of people are the things that make them unclean. All these evil things begin inside people, in the mind: evil thoughts, sexual sins, stealing, murder, adultery, greed, evil actions, lying, doing sinful things, jealousy, speaking evil of others, pride, and foolish living. All these evil things come from inside and make people unclean" (NCV).

The moment you decide to change your thinking, not just talking but doing it for real; your life, perspective and concerns will change. Don't complain about what you won't change. If you like it then keep the act to yourself. Some of us need to get tired of ourselves enough to change for the better.

DEVOTION 7

Proverbs 18:21 NLT:

The tongue can bring death or life; those who love to talk will reap the consequences.

Too often, too many of us are just down right negative. It seems that we often only speak the worst, mostly because we often think the worst. We make a simple situation into a life-threatening issue, we're something like the side-effects on medicine commercials. They go from speaking about how a medicine is so great for us, and the next thing we know, there's a voice speaking about how this medicine 'could' do so many terrible things when taken - scary thing to hear when you're the patient taking the medicine. Well, that's so often how we allow the enemy to play on our minds. He becomes such a tiny fast speaking voice that we listen to and we begin to repeat what he's saying. The only difference is that he's not into saying what it 'could' cause, he's forcing what it will do. This situation 'will' cause you drama, fear, dysfunction, too quit, to lose, illnesses and so much more. Immediately, we take the side effects over the promises.

How often has God used the Holy Spirit to speak life and it becomes factual that you have the job, the house, the car, and the business, but instantly you begin to think; *my credit isn't as good, credentials don't match, I can't afford* - and your sunshine turns to a storm in your mind. If you change your 'stinkin thinkin' you change your whole life. As I was writing this devotion the song played in my mind *'there's nothing my/your/our God can NOT do and won't for that matter'*. He's so amazing but do we believe that there's nothing He can't and more so won't do for us? But, here it comes. Who will you trust? Whose voice will be put to rest in your mental commercial?

Today's devotion is a challenge for you to speak life over every situation. Not just for you, but for your family and friends. Too often we're so used to mess, drama, negativity, jealousy, malice and hatred that it becomes our first thoughts on everything. We will talk ourselves out of the win. Say: "I will be a wife", your last marriage has nothing to do with what and who God has for you. "I will be a homeowner" your credit doesn't prevent Gods approval. "I will graduate". "I will feel great today". "My kids are successful". "My father will be healed". "Addiction won't take over my children". "Generational and ancestral curses won't win within my life". "Poverty and struggles are denounced over my life". What are you speaking daily and believing? Speak what you desire.

Do not be afraid of them; the LORD your God Himself will fight for you." **Deut. 3:22**

As I slept last night, a picture came clearly to my mind. Is it that we are disobedient or not knowledgeable often when it comes to what God says He will do for us. It was a clear picture of last weekend's fight, with Floyd Mayweather winning once again with a TKO. It struck me as odd that we make plans to bid on Floyd, have parties, and go above and beyond trusting that he will continue to be the reigning boxing champ. People love his arrogance and his confidence and often never doubt his ability to consistently win.

But, I suppose that what really struck me in my rest was that we have a word above that states the same for us from God. It's no guessing or wondering. We can bid with faith, knowing that He stated that He WILL fight for YOU, ME, US, and that His record is for sure flawless and undefeated. The good thing about God is that He has no chance of losing, but many of us will place more faith in Floyd than in God. I feel we need to get out of our flesh for a minute, go back through our lives, replay fights and really dissect them, and realize that God truly has been on a winning streak for us. The thing is we get so caught up in the fight we are in now. We hear the enemy speaking loud and clear like McGregor was, about how our finances aren't enough, how our kids are going to continue to show out and disappoint, how our friends are nowhere to be found when we need them, how our jobs seem to be stressing us out, how our cars are giving us issues, how our relationships are on the brinks of failure, how illness is so close, pregnancy is a struggle, how we're not moving up like we feel we should, and so on and so forth. We could all keep adding the things the enemy is giving the promoter of our current fight - as God sits as did Mayweather and never utters a word. See, when you're confident in your skill and know your track record, technique, and opponent, you're not easily moved nor shaken. You're constantly waiting for the WIN.

So, as we apply today's word we must truly not be afraid, not worry, not get off track, not wonder, but wait on the TKO. We must to truly go back and look at every fight He has won for us. Now we may have had to go after a few rounds, we may have had a few bumps and bruises, but He's never been one to lose on our behalf. We must be wise, by not trying to jump into the ring and taking over the fight.

We're bound to be knocked out by distractions, discouragement, hurt, and overwhelming thoughts, but that's truly when you need to apply the word to your situation. But, how can we be equipped to fight with the full armor if we don't have a word. Google a word that applies to what you're going through. We're willing to google everything else, seek social media's counsel and even contact our friends for a fight God has already won. Why would I not contact the one who is most knowledgeable about my situation and opponents? I think we get confused trying to control the fight when we should be more focused on God winning it.

DEVOTION 8

Prayer Devotions

Dear Gracious Heavenly Father, today we come asking that you give us the faith and knowledge to know that you will fight for us in all our situations. Help us to understand that you're undefeated and never failing in our fights, and that we can step back knowing a TKO is coming. We can't get weary or lose our momentum of trusting you because it seems we're taking some tough punches and have been knocked down a few rounds - help us to know and believe that's when you're strengthening us, helping us to endure, and getting us stronger and more equipped for what's to come.

DEVOTION 9

Ring the Alarm...

We've all heard the storm alarms go off in the city here or there. We've even heard the ones that sound on the television and on the radio that tell us this is a monthly test. Wouldn't life be great if God rang the life alarm when a storm was about to hit your life, or our plans were about to be rerouted.

Depression... *Rinnggg.* Stress. *Rinnggg...* Financial Issues....*Rinnngg.* Sickness in our family...*Ringgg..*

Relationship failures.... *Ringggg..*Staff Issues....*Ring...* Boy, what if life would give us a heads up and we'd be better prepared to handle the situation, or would we? Because our plans aren't always Gods plans.

Too often we try and plan our lives and prep for what's to come, but life doesn't always work out how we plan for it to. We plan to marry and live happily ever after, be wealthy and never struggle, go to college and have the dream job, get the nice car, run a smooth business, have kids who never have any issues, and watch our parents and siblings live forever. How many of these plans were yours and ended up in another direction?

Despite the most careful planning, the Road of Life is unpredictable. We might have driving directions from our GPS, but at times life throws a detour that may take us towards an unforeseen roadblock that can deter us. Then what?

Happily, Ever After, Does it ever happen? It never occurred to me that God might be waiting for His 'happily ever after' too. God too may think that some of His plans have not gone as He wanted and that we were laughing at Him. It all started with Adam and Eve. They had only one rule, and they broke it. Cain killed Abel. The Israelites begged to return to Egypt. Moses broke the first set of the Ten Commandments. God plans, but the rules aren't always kept by us. No sex before marriage. Thou shall not lie. We shouldn't have done or said that. Don't abort that baby.

Our best-laid out plans in life can be bumped by unexpected changes, which could be either disappointing or exciting. Personal or other setbacks, losses of loved ones, illnesses or accidents, broken hearts or torture are not uncommon occurrences in our lives. On the other hand, fate can provide unanticipated good fortune or heartening experiences to help us through everything. Just trust God in it all. After all, what has worry cured for you?

Even in dark times however, we know at some level that 'this too shall pass'. After the terrible feelings, we MUST gather our thoughts, bring our strengths to an all-time new, *and we do overcome because we must*. Currently, remember that time will eventually make things better.

In addition to 'death and taxes' which are life's inevitabilities, there is another experience you can bet the house on—'stuff' will for sure happen in our lives, unexpected changes will occur. Rest assured, however, that after extreme joy or deep sorrow, your life will return to its natural state of being healed, sooner than later. Today, trust God's plan no matter how horrible the day goes, how many setbacks occur, or how many people cancel or call in. Trust that God has a perfect plan for YOU.

Say your prayers... Amen

DEDICATIONS

This book is dedicated to several important people. My first dedication is Kinsley Arielle McCaulley. We were supposed to have a baby but instead we had an angel. I may never get to hold you again. But, you will always be in my heart and in my every day thoughts. I'm thankful for the time I had with you and will forever be grateful for what it taught me. I never would have guessed when I was preparing to birth you my angel that you wouldn't live, but God also saw fit for me to birth this book as we planned. You were Too beautiful for earth, but you will forever have a place in my heart. Love you Kin watch over us daily.

To my three boys Fredrick, Ethan and Achtyn I'm thankful for the love and care you show me as a mother. Too see the type of unconditional love you three exhibit is more than a blessing. To love no matter my financial status, what I can give you, how I've stumbled in life you sill exhibit genuine love. Each one of you have made your own impression on my life, that inspired this book. I can never thank you three enough. Ill forever push you to be the best men you can be. I'll always speak life into you and never will I ever stop loving you. Forever grateful the mom of three great young men. Because of you I'm now able to Help someone else. Mommy Loves you!

To Kody McCaulley it's not what a person shows you when everything is good, but what they reveal in your toughest times. I will forever be thankful for you for the experiences and for the times you stood by me in my darkest hour. My appreciation is forever extended to you. To be as strong as you've been through the death our daughter for me has been a true blessing. During my most vulnerable stage you've loved the person that I've shown you, you've pushed the person who didn't think she could make it. And most of all you loved the person who felt love could no longer exist. To see the example of love you've shown me has proven love heals. Thanks for loving the woman that I am without stipulations or conditions. I pray that God continues to bless you!

To my friends, supporters and family Thanks for the love and continuous prayers. You will always be in my heart and on my mind. Not a day goes by that God doesn't push me through one of you being obedient through speaking a word when I want to give up. This shows me I'm doing what God has called me to do. Forever grateful for each of you.

To my parents I can never repay you guys for you love and support. Life has shown me so much and through your raising and pushing me I am who I am and where I am because God blessed me with you. Thanks for never judging but knowing me and allowing me that flaws and all. Lastly, Thanks for incorporating my mom into our lives and as she rests in peace I know she loved me and you all always made sure I knew it.

To you I know that this is a tough time for us. We planned so much for our babies and in the blink of an eye God showed us his plan for Kinsley. But, remember the same God who has kept us in all our tough situations will keep us through this. We've gone through so much and we've always come out stronger and better. Your prayers, love and continuous support has been appreciated. I realize we can do so much more together than apart.

AUTHOR

M el Bowers, the mom, the friend, the mentor, the entrepreneur that is me. Today, I'm thankful not just for the good days in my life but for all the lessons. Each lesson has molded each season in my life to allow me to share my heart with you. I ask today that you not judge but have an open mind to be honest and heal. From every mistake, to every come back I know they all molded me to write this book in total transparency. I pray that this book will Help someone who has been suffering and going through. This wasn't just for the readers. This book, the experience and all the tears were also for me. I will continue to pray that God births remarkable things for me to give his people. I will forever be thankful for life and the blessings and burdens. I have scars and have some bumps in the road. Never allow the enemy to convince you that life can't be fixed by our awesome God.